# The Wisdom of James Allen

# The Wisdom of James Allen

## Five Books in One

- As a Man Thinketh
- The Path to Prosperity
- The Mastery of Destiny
- The Way of Peace
- Entering the Kingdom

Laurel Creek Press
San Diego, California 2001

Laurel Creek Press is an imprint of Blue Dove Press.

For a free 68-Page catalog featuring inspirational works from the world'
religions and spiritual traditions, Contact:
    The Blue Dove Foundation
    4204 Sorrento Valley Blvd, Suite K
    San Diego, CA 92121
    858-623-3330 or 800-691-1008
    www.bluedove.org

The Wisdom of James Allen
    Edited by Andy Zupko. This book contains the complete and
    unabridged text of each of the five listed works, with the
    exception of a few poems. For clarity, some obscure or archaic
    English words and phrases were rendered into modern usage.
    James Allen used the generic masculine in his writings, as was
    the common practice of his time.

© 1997    Second printing - 2000

ISBN: 1-889606-00-6

Cover and Text Design: Brian Moucka


Library of Congress Cataloging-in-Publication Data
Allen, James, 1864-1912.
    The wisdom of James Allen : five books in one / James Allen
        p. cm.
    ISBN 1-889606-00-6 (perfect bound)
        1. New Thought. I. Title

BF639 .A672 2000
289.9'8--dc21
                                00-061207

# About James Allen

JAMES ALLEN has been called the "literary mystery man" of the twentieth century. Although his best-selling classic *As A Man Thinketh* has inspired millions around the world, little is known about the author himself.

What is known about Allen is that he was born in 1864 in Leicester, England. His father was a well-to-do businessman who, because of poor economic conditions, went bankrupt in 1878 and was tragically murdered one year later. This required James to leave school at the age of fifteen to help support his family. Allen eventually married and became a personal secretary for an executive of a large English corporation.

At the age of 38 he reached what can be called a crossroads in his life. Influenced by the writings of Tolstoy, Allen came to the realization that a life devoted to making money and spending it on frivolous activities was a meaningless way to live. He retired from his employment and moved with his wife to a small cottage on the southwest shore of England to pursue a life of contemplation. It was here at Iltracombe that Allen pursued his dream of voluntary poverty, spiritual self-discipline and a life of simplicity as taught by his mentor, Tolstoy.

A typical Allen day would be to rise very early in the morning and walk to a bluff overlooking the ocean, where he would remain in meditation for an hour or so. And as the cobwebs which had obscured his spiritual vision lifted, the secrets of the universe would unfold before him. Quietly these impressions would be recorded within. Afterwards, he would return home and pen his insights on paper. Afternoons were committed to tending his garden; evenings to communion with townsfolk who wished to discuss loftier philosophical issues.

For ten years Allen led this quiet, pensive life, earning a small stipend from royalties paid on his writing. Then suddenly, at the age of 48, Allen passed away. He died the way he lived, a virtual unknown, untouched by fame, unrewarded by fortune. It would only be afterwards that the literary world would come to recognize the genius and inspiration of his work. But this is the way the anonymous English mystic would have wanted it—to posthumously share his spiritual insights with the world.

Allen's classic work, *As A Man Thinketh*, as well as *The Path to Prosperity*, *The Way of Peace*, *The Mastery of Destiny* and *Entering the Kingdom*, have all been combined to bring you *The Wisdom of James Allen*. It is his final, loving bequest to the world.

# Foreword

I LOOKED AROUND UPON THE WORLD, and saw that it was shadowed by sorrow and scorched by the fierce fires of suffering. And I looked for the cause. I looked around, but I could not find it; I looked in books, but I could not find it; I looked within, and found there both the cause and the self-made nature of that cause. I looked again, and deeper, and found the remedy. I found one Law, the Law of Love; one Life, the life of adjustment to that Law; one Truth, the Truth of a conquered mind and a quiet and obedient heart.

And I dreamed of writing books which would help men and women, whether rich or poor, learned or unlearned, worldly or unworldly to find within themselves the source of all success, all happiness, all accomplishment, all truth. And the dream remained with me, and at last became substantial; and now I send forth these books into the world on a mission of healing and blessedness, knowing that they cannot fail to reach the homes and hearts of those who are waiting and ready to receive them.

*James Allen*

# CONTENTS:

# The Wisdom
of James Allen

# As a Man Thinketh

*Mind is the Master-power that molds and makes,*
*And Man is Mind, and evermore he takes*
*The tool of Thought, and shaping what he wills,*
*Brings forth a thousand joys, a thousand ills:—*
*He thinks in secret, and it comes to pass:*
*Environment is but his looking-glass.*

# TABLE OF CONTENTS

# Thought & Character

THE APHORISM, "As a man thinketh in his heart, so is he," embraces the whole of man's being, but is so comprehensive that it reaches out to every condition and circumstance of life. A man is literally what he thinks, his character being the complete sum of all his thoughts.

As the plant springs from, and could not be without, the seed, so every act of a man springs from the hidden seeds of thought and could not have appeared without them. This applies equally to those acts called "spontaneous" and "unpremeditated" as to those which are deliberately executed.

Act is the blossom of thought, and joy and suffering are its fruits; thus does a man harvest the sweet and bitter fruitage of his own husbandry.

*Thought in the mind*
*Hath made us what we are*

*By thought was wrought and built.*
*If a man's mind*
*Hath evil thoughts,*
*Pain comes on him*
*As comes the wheel the ox behind...*
*If one endure in purity of thought,*
*Joy follows him*
*As his own shadow-sure.*

Man is a growth by law, and not a creation by artifice, and cause and effect is as absolute and undeviating in the hidden realm of thought as in the world of visible and material things.

A noble character and God-like character is not a thing of favor or chance, but is the natural result of a continued effort in right thinking, the effect of long-cherished association with God-like thought. An ignoble and bestial character, by the same process, is the result of the continued harboring of groveling thoughts.

### You Are Master of Your Fate

Man is made or unmade by himself; in the armory of thought he forges the weapons by which he destroys himself; he also fashions the tools with which he builds for himself heavenly mansions of joy and strength and peace. By the right choice and true application of thought, man ascends to the Divine Perfection; by the abuse and wrong application of thought, he descends below the level of the beast. Between these two extremes are all the grades of character, and man is their maker and master.

Of all the beautiful truths pertaining to the soul, none is more gladdening or fruitful of divine promise and confidence than this—that man is the master of thought, the molder of character, and the maker and shaper of condition, environment, and destiny.

As a being of Power, Intelligence, and Love, and the lord of his own thoughts, man holds the key to every situation, and contains within himself that transforming and regenerative agency by which he makes himself what he wills.

Man is always the master, even in his weakness and most abandoned state; but in his weakness and degradation he is the foolish master who misgoverns his "household." When he begins to reflect upon his condition, and to search diligently for the Law upon which his being is established, he then becomes the wise master directing his energies with intelligence, and fashioning his thoughts to fruitful issues.

Such is the *conscious* master, and man can only thus become by discovering *within himself* the laws of thought, which discovery is totally a matter of application, self-analysis, and experience.

## Seek and You Shall Find

Only by much searching and mining are gold and diamonds obtained, and man can find every truth connected with his being if he will dig deep into the mine of his soul.

Man is the maker of his character, the molder of his life, and the builder of his destiny. This he may prove unerringly, if he will watch, control, and alter his thoughts, tracing their effects upon himself, upon others, and upon his life and circumstances; this he may prove by linking cause and effect by patient practice and investigation and utilizing his every experience, even to the most trivial, everyday occurrence, as a means of obtaining that knowledge of himself which is Understanding, Wisdom, Power.

In this direction, as in no other, is the law absolute that "He that seeketh findeth; and to him that knocketh it shall be opened"; for only by patience, practice and ceaseless persistence can a man enter the Door of the Temple of Knowledge.

# Effect of Thought
# on Circumstances

A MAN'S MIND MAY BE LIKENED TO A GARDEN, which may be intelligently cultivated or allowed to run wild; but whether cultivated or neglected, it must and will, bring forth. If no useful seeds are put into it, then an abundance of useless weed seeds will fall into it, and will continue to produce their worthless kind.

Just as a gardener cultivates his plot, keeping it free from weeds, and growing the flowers and fruits which he requires, so may a man tend the garden of his mind, weeding out all the wrong, useless, and impure thoughts, and cultivating toward perfection the flowers and fruits of right, useful, and pure thoughts.

By this process, a man sooner or later discovers that he is the master gardener of his soul, the director of his life. He also reveals, within himself, the laws of thought, and understands, with ever-increasing accuracy, how the thought-forces and mind-elements operate in the shaping his character, circumstances, and destiny.

Thought and character are one, and as character can only manifest and discover itself through environment and circumstance, the outer conditions of a person's life will always be found to be harmoniously related to his inner state. This does not mean that a man's circumstances at any given time are an indication of his *entire* character, but that those circumstances are so intimately connected with some vital thought-element within him that, for the time being, they are indispensable to his development.

Every man is where he is by the law of his being; the thoughts which he has built into his character have brought him there, and in the arrangement of his life there is no element of chance. All is the result of a law which cannot err. This is just as true of those who feel "out of harmony" with their surroundings as of those who are contented with them.

### Circumstances Grow Out of Thoughts

As a progressive and evolving being, man is

where he is that he may learn that he may grow; and as he learns the spiritual lesson which any circumstance contains for him, it passes away to other circumstances.

Man is buffeted by circumstances so long as he believes himself to be the creature of outside conditions. But when he realizes that he is a creative power, and that he may command the hidden soil and seeds of his being out of which circumstances grow, he then becomes the rightful master of himself.

That circumstances *grow* out of thought every man knows who has for any length of time practiced self-control and self-purification for he will have noticed that the alteration of his circumstances has been in exact ratio with his altered mental condition. So true is this that when a man earnestly applies himself to remedy the defects in his character, and makes swift and marked progress, he passes rapidly through a succession of vicissitudes.

The soul attracts that which it secretly harbors; that which it loves, and also that which it fears; it reaches the height of its cherished aspirations; it falls to the level of its unchastened desires—and circumstances are the means by which the soul receives its own.

Every thought-seed sown or allowed to fall into the mind, and to take root there, produces its own, blossoming sooner or later into act, and bearing its own fruit of opportunity and circumstance. Good thoughts bear good fruit, bad thoughts bad fruit.

The outer world of circumstance shapes itself to the inner world of thought, and both pleasant and unpleasant external conditions are factors which make for the ultimate good of the individual. As the reaper of his own harvest, man learns both by suffering and bliss.

Following the inmost desires, aspirations, and thoughts by which he allows himself to be dominated (pursuing the will-o'-the-wisps of impure imaginings or steadfastly walking the highway of strong and high endeavor), a man at last arrives at their fruition and fulfillment in the outer conditions of his life. The laws of growth and adjustment are everywhere in effect.

### Justice is Exact

A man does not come to destitution or prison through the tyranny of fate or circumstance, but by the pathway of groveling thoughts and base desires. Nor does a pure-minded man fall suddenly into crime by stress of any mere external force. The criminal thought had long been secretly fostered in the heart, and the hour of opportunity revealed its gathered power. Circumstance does not make the man; it reveals him to himself. No such conditions can exist in a man as vice and its attendant sufferings apart from vicious inclinations, or ascending into virtue and its pure happiness without the continued cultivation of virtuous aspirations. Man, therefore, as the lord and master of thought, is the maker of himself, the shaper and author of environment.

Even at birth the soul comes to its own and through every step of its earthly pilgrimage it attracts those combinations of conditions which reveal itself, which are the reflections of its own purity and impurity, its strength and weakness.

Men do not attract that which they *want*, but that which they *are*. Their whims, fancies, and ambitions are thwarted at every step, but their inmost thoughts and desires are fed with their own food, be it foul or clean. The "divinity that shapes our ends" is in ourselves; it is our very self. Man is manacled only by himself. Thought and action are the jailers of Fate— they imprison, being base; they are also the angels of Freedom—they liberate, being noble. Not what he wishes and prays for does a man get, but what he justly earns. His wishes and prayers are only gratified and answered when they harmonize with his thoughts and actions.

In the light of this truth, what, then, is the meaning of "fighting against circumstances"? It means that man is continually revolting against an *effect* without, while all the time he is nourishing and preserving its *cause* in his heart. That cause may take the form of a conscious vice or an unconscious weakness; but whatever it is, it stubbornly retards the efforts of its possessor, and calls aloud for remedy.

### Three Examples of Ignorance

Men are anxious to improve their circumstances, but are unwilling to improve themselves; they therefore remain bound. The man who does not shrink from self-crucifixion can never fail to accomplish the object upon which his heart is set. This is as true of earthly as of heavenly things. Even the man whose sole object is to acquire wealth must be prepared to make great personal sacrifices before he can accomplish his object; and how much more so he who would achieve a strong and well-poised life?

Here is a man who is wretchedly poor. He is

extremely anxious that his surroundings and home comforts should be improved, yet he continually shirks his work, and considers he is justified in trying to deceive his employer on the ground of insufficiency of his wages. Such a man does not understand the simplest rudiments of true prosperity. He is not only totally unfitted to rise out of his wretchedness, but he is actually attracting to himself a still deeper wretchedness, by dwelling in, and acting out, indolent, deceptive, and unmanly thoughts.

Here is a rich man who is the victim of a painful and persistent disease as the result of gluttony. He is willing to give large sums of money to get rid of it, but he will not sacrifice his gluttonous desires. He wants to gratify his taste for rich and unnatural foods and have his health as well. Such a man is totally unfit to have health, because he has not yet learned the first principles of a healthy life.

Here is an employer who adopts crooked measures to avoid paying the regulation wage, and, in the hope of making larger profits, reduces the wages of his workers. Such a man is altogether unfitted for prosperity, and when he finds himself bankrupt, both as regards reputation and riches, he blames circumstances, not knowing that he is the sole author of his condition.

I have introduced these three cases merely as illustrative of the truth that man is the cause (though nearly always unconsciously) of circumstances, and that, while aiming at a good end, he is continually frustrating its accomplishment by encouraging thoughts and desires which cannot possibly harmonize with that end. Such cases could be multiplied and varied almost indefinitely, but this is not necessary, as the reader can, if he so resolves, trace the action of the laws of thought in his own mind and life, and until this is done, mere external facts cannot serve as a ground of reasoning.

### Good Cannot Produce Evil

Circumstances, however, are so complicated, thought is so deeply rooted, and the conditions of happiness vary so vastly with individuals, that a man's *entire* soul condition (although it may be known to himself) cannot be judged by another from the external aspect of his life alone. A man may be honest in certain directions, yet suffer privations; as a man may be dishonest in certain directions, yet acquire wealth.

The conclusion usually formed that one man fails *because of his particular honesty*, and another prospers *because of his particular dishonesty*, is the result of superficial judgement, which assumes that the dishonest man is almost totally corrupt, and the honest man almost entirely virtuous. In the light of deeper knowledge and wider experience, such judgement is found to be erroneous.

The dishonest man may have some admirable virtues the other does not possess, and the honest man obnoxious vices which are absent in the other. The honest man reaps the good results of his honest thoughts and acts; he also brings upon himself the sufferings which his vices produce. The dishonest man likewise harvests his own suffering and happiness.

It is pleasing to human vanity to believe that we suffer because of one's virtue; but not until a man roots out every sickly, bitter, and impure thought from his mind, and washes every sinful stain from his soul, can he be in a position to know and declare that his sufferings are the result of his good, and not of his bad qualities.

And on the way to, yet long before he has reached that supreme perfection, he will have found, working in his mind and life, the Great Law which is absolutely just, and which cannot, therefore, give good for evil, evil for good. Possessed of such knowledge, he will then know, looking back upon his past ignorance and blindness, that his life is, and always was, justly ordered, and that all his past experiences, good and bad, were the equitable outworking of his evolving, yet unevolved self.

## You Are What You Think

Good thoughts and actions can never produce bad results; bad thoughts and actions can never produce good results. This is but saying that nothing can come from corn but corn, nothing from nettles but nettles. Men understand this law in the natural world, and work with it; but few understand it in the mental and moral world (though its operation there is just as simple and undeviating), and they, therefore, do not cooperate with it.

Suffering is *always* the effect of wrong thought in some direction. It is an indication that the individual is out of harmony with himself, with the Law of his being. The sole and supreme use of suffering is to purify, to burn out all that is useless and impure. Suffering ceases for him who is pure. There is no object in burning gold after the dross has been removed, and a perfectly pure and enlightened being could not suffer.

The circumstances which a man encounters with suffering are the result of his own mental disharmony. The circumstances which a man encounters with blessedness are the result of his own mental harmony. Blessedness, not material possessions, is the measure of right thought; wretchedness, not lack of material possessions, is the measure of wrong thought. A man may be cursed and rich; he may be blessed and poor. Blessedness and riches are only joined together when the riches are rightly and wisely used, and the poor man only descends into wretchedness when he regards his lot as a burden unjustly imposed.

Lack and excess are the two extremes of wretchedness. They are both equally unnatural and the result of mental disorder. A man is not rightly conditioned until he is a happy, healthy, and prosperous being; and happiness, health and prosperity are the result of a harmonious adjustment of the inner with the outer, of the man with his surroundings.

## Discover the Hidden Powers Within

A man only begins to be a man when he ceases to whine and revile, and commences to search for the hidden justice which regulates his life. And when he adapts his mind to that regulating factor, he ceases to accuse others as the cause of his condition, and builds himself up in strong and noble thoughts; ceases to kick against circumstances, but begins to *use* them as aids to his more rapid progress, and as a means of discovering the hidden powers and possibilities within himself.

Law, not confusion, is the dominating principle of the universe. Justice, not injustice, is the soul and substance of life. Righteousness, not corruption, is the molding and moving force in the spiritual government of the world. This being so, man has but to right himself to find that the universe is right; and during the process of putting himself right, he will find that as he alters his thoughts towards things and other people, things and other people will alter towards him.

The proof of this truth is in every person, and it therefore admits of easy investigation by systematic introspection and self-analysis. Let a man radically alter his thoughts, and he will be astonished at the rapid transformation it will effect in the material conditions of his life.

### The Aftermath of Corrupt Thoughts

Men imagine that thought can be kept secret,

but it cannot; it rapidly crystallizes into habit, **and** habit solidifies into circumstance.

- Bestial thoughts crystallize into habits of drunkenness and sensuality, which solidify into circumstances of destitution and disease.

- Impure thoughts of every kind crystallize into enervating and confusing habits, which solidify into distracting and adverse circumstances.

- Thoughts of fear, doubt, and indecision crystallize into weak, unmanly, and irresolute habits which solidify into circumstances of failure, lack, and slavish dependence.

- Lazy thoughts crystallize into habits of uncleanliness and dishonesty, which solidify into circumstances of foulness and beggary.

- Hateful and condemnatory thoughts crystallize into habits of accusation and violence, which solidify into circumstances of injury and persecution.

- Selfish thoughts of all kinds crystallize into habits of self-seeking, which solidify into circumstances more or less distressing.

### The Aftermath of Beautiful Thoughts

On the other hand, beautiful thoughts of all

kinds crystallize into habits of grace and kindliness, which solidify into friendly and sunny circumstances:

- Pure thoughts crystallize into habits of temperance and self-control, which solidify into circumstances of repose and peace.
- Thoughts of courage, self-reliance, and decision crystallize into manly habits, which solidify into circumstances of success, plenty and freedom.
- Energetic thoughts crystallize into habits of cleanliness and industry, which solidify into circumstances of pleasantness and peace.
- Gentle and forgiving thoughts crystallize into habits of gentleness, which solidify into protective and preservative circumstances.
- Loving and unselfish thoughts crystallize into habits of self-forgetfulness for others, which solidify into circumstances of sure and abiding prosperity and true riches.

### Thoughts Shape Your Circumstances

A particular train of thought persisted in, be it good or bad, cannot fail to produce its results on the character and circumstances. A man cannot directly choose his circumstances, but he can choose his thoughts, and so indirectly, yet surely, shape his circumstances.

Nature helps every man to the gratification of the thoughts which he most encourages, and opportunities are presented which will most speedily bring to the surface both the good and evil thoughts.

Let a man cease from his sinful thoughts, and all the world will soften towards him, and be ready to help him; let him put away his weakly and sickly thoughts, and lo! opportunities will spring up on every hand to aid his strong resolves. Let him encourage good thoughts, and no hard fate shall bind him down to wretchedness and shame.

The world is your kaleidoscope, and the varying combinations of colors which at every succeeding moment it presents to you are the exquisitely adjusted pictures of your ever-moving thoughts.

*You will be what you will be;*
*Let failure find its false content*
*In the poor world, 'environment,'*
*But spirit scorns it, and is free.*

*It masters time, it conquers space;*
*It cows that boastful trickster Chance,*
*And bids the tyrant Circumstance*

*Uncrown, and fill a servant's place.*

*The human Will, that force unseen,*
*The offspring of a deathless Soul,*
*Can hew a way to any goal,*
*Through walls of granite intervene.*

*Be patient in delay,*
*But wait as one who understands;*
*When spirit rises and commands,*
*The gods are ready to obey.*

# Effect of Thought
# on Health and the Body

THE BODY IS THE SERVANT OF THE MIND. It obeys the operations of the mind, whether they be deliberately chosen or automatically expressed. At the bidding of unlawful thoughts the body sinks rapidly into disease and decay; at the command of glad and beautiful thoughts it becomes clothed with youthfulness and beauty.

Disease and health, like circumstances, are rooted in thought. Sickly thoughts will express themselves through a sickly body. Thoughts of fear have been known to kill a man as speedily as a bullet, and they are continually killing thousands of people just as surely though less rapidly. The people who live in fear of disease are the people who get it. Anxiety quickly demoralizes the whole body, and lays it open to the entrance of disease; while impure thoughts, even if not physically indulged, soon will shatter the nervous system.

Strong, pure, and happy thoughts build up the body in vigor and grace. The body is a delicate and pliable instrument, which responds readily to thoughts by which it is impressed, and habits of thought will produce their own effects, good or bad, upon it.

Men will continue to have impure and poisoned blood as long as they propagate unclean thoughts. Out of a clean heart comes a clean life and a clean body. Out of a defiled mind proceeds a defiled life and a corrupt body. Thought is the fountain of action, life, and manifestation; make the fountain pure, and all will be pure.

Change of diet will not help a man who will not change his thoughts. When a man makes his thoughts pure, he no longer desires impure food.

Clean thoughts make clean habits. The so-called saint who does not wash his body is not a saint. He who has strengthened and purified his thoughts does not need to consider the malevolent microbe.

### Your Mind Determines Your Health

If you would perfect your body, guard your mind. If you would renew your body, beautify your mind.

Thoughts of malice, envy, disappointment, despondency, rob the body of its health and grace. A sour face does not come by chance; it is made by sour thoughts. Wrinkles that mar are drawn by folly, passion, pride.

I know a woman of ninety-six who has the bright, innocent face of a girl. I know a man well under middle age whose face is drawn into inharmonious contours. The one is the result of a sweet and sunny disposition; the other is the outcome of passion and discontent.

As you cannot have a sweet and wholesome home unless you admit the air and sunshine freely into your rooms, so a strong body and a bright, happy, or serene countenance can only result from the free admittance of thoughts of joy and good will and serenity.

On the faces of the aged there are wrinkles made by sympathy; others wrought by strong and pure thought, and others carved by passion: who cannot distinguish them? With those who have lived righteously, age is calm, peaceful, and softly mellowed, like the setting sun. I have recently seen a philosopher on his deathbed. He was not old except in years. He died as sweetly and peacefully as he had lived.

There is no physician like a cheerful thought for dissipating the ills of the body; there is no comforter to compare with good will for dispersing the shadows of grief and sorrow. To live continually in thoughts of ill will, cynicism, suspicion, and envy, is to be confined to a self-made prison. But to think well of all, to be cheerful with all, to patiently learn to find the good in all—such unselfish thoughts are the very portals of heaven; and to dwell day by day in thoughts of peace toward every creature will bring abounding peace to their possessor.

# Thought & Purpose

U NTIL THOUGHT IS LINKED WITH PURPOSE there is no intelligent accomplishment. With the majority the ship of thought is allowed to "drift" upon the ocean of life. Aimlessness is a common vice, and such drifting must not continue for him who would steer clear of catastrophe and destruction.

They who have no central purpose in their life fall easy prey to petty worries, fears, troubles, and self-pityings, all of which are indications of weakness, which lead, just as surely as deliberately planned sins (though by a different route), to failure, unhappiness, and loss, for weakness cannot persist in a power-evolving universe.

A man should conceive of a legitimate purpose in his heart, and set out to accomplish it. He should make this purpose the centralizing point of his thoughts. It may take the form of a spiritual ideal, or it may be a worldly object according to his nature at the time being; but whatever it is, he should steadily focus his thought forces upon the object which he has set before him.

He should make this purpose his supreme duty, and should devote himself to its attainment, not allowing his thoughts to wander into fleeting fancies, longings, and imaginings. This is the royal road to self-control and true concentration of thought.

Even if he fails again and again to accomplish his purpose (as he necessarily must until weakness is overcome), the *strength of character gained* will be the measure of his *true* success, and this will form a starting-point in his life for future power and triumph.

Those who are not prepared for the apprehension of a *great* purpose should fix their thoughts upon the faultless performance of their duty, no matter how insignificant their task may appear. Only in this way can the thoughts be gathered and focused, and resolution and energy be developed, which being done, there is nothing which may not be accomplished.

### Strength Grows with Purpose

The weakest soul, knowing its own weakness,

and believing this truth—that strength can only be developed by effort and practice, will, thus believing, at once begin to exert itself. And by adding effort to effort, patience to patience, and strength to strength, will never cease to develop, and will at last grow divinely strong.

As the physically weak man can make himself strong by careful and patient training, so the man of weak thoughts can make them strong by exercising himself in right thinking.

To put away aimlessness and weakness, and to begin to think with purpose, is to enter the ranks of those strong ones who only recognize failure as one of the pathways to attainment; who make all conditions serve them, and who think strongly, attempt fearlessly, and accomplish masterfully.

Having conceived of his purpose, a man should mentally mark out a *straight* pathway to its achievement, looking neither to the right nor the left. Doubts and fears should be rigorously excluded. They are disintegrating elements which break up the straight line of effort, rendering it crooked, ineffectual, useless. Thoughts of doubt and fear never accomplish anything, and never can. They always lead to failure. Purpose, energy, power to do, and all strong thoughts cease when doubt and fear creep in.

## *Eliminate Doubt and Fear*

The will to do springs from the knowledge that we can do. Doubt and fear are the great enemies of knowledge, and he who encourages them, who does not slay them, thwarts himself at every step.

He who has conquered doubt and fear has conquered failure. His every thought is allied with power, and all difficulties are bravely met and wisely overcome. His purposes are seasonably planted, and they bloom and bring forth fruit which does not fall prematurely to the ground.

Thought allied fearlessly to purpose becomes creative force. He who knows this is ready to become something higher and stronger than a mere bundle of wavering thoughts and fluctuating sensations; he who does this has become the conscious and intelligent wielder of his mental powers.

# The Thought
# Factor in Achievement

ALL THAT A MAN ACHIEVES and all that he fails to achieve is the direct result of his own thoughts. In a justly ordered universe, where loss of equipoise would mean total destruction, individual responsibility must be absolute. A man's weakness and strength, purity and impurity, are his own, and not another man's. They are brought about by himself and not by another; and they can only be altered by himself, never by another. His condition is also his own, and not another man's. His suffering and his happiness are evolved from within. As he thinks, so he is; as he continues to think, so he remains.

A strong man cannot help a weaker unless that weaker is *willing* to be helped, and even then the weak man must become strong of himself. He must, by his own efforts, develop the strength which he admires in another. None but himself can alter his condition.

It has been usual for men to think and to say, "Many men are slaves because one is an oppressor; let us hate the oppressor." Now, however, there is amongst an increasing few a tendency to reverse this judgement and to say, "One man is an oppressor because many are slaves; let us despise the slaves."

The truth is that the oppressor and slave are cooperators in ignorance, and, while seeming to afflict each other, are in reality afflicting themselves. A perfect Knowledge perceives the action of law in the weakness of the oppressed and the misapplied power of the oppressor. A perfect Love seeing the suffering which both states entail and condemns neither. A perfect Compassion embraces oppressor and oppressed.

He who has conquered weakness, and has put away all selfish thoughts, belongs neither to oppressor nor oppressed. He is free.

A man can only rise, conquer, and achieve by lifting up his thoughts. He can only remain weak, and abject, and miserable, by refusing to lift up his thoughts.

## *There is No Progress Without Sacrifice*

Before a man can achieve anything, even in worldly things, he must lift his thoughts above slavish animal indulgence. He may not, in order to succeed, necessarily give up *all* animality and selfishness, by any means; but a portion of it must, at least, be sacrificed.

A man whose first thought is bestial indulgence could neither think clearly nor plan methodically; he could not find and develop his latent resources, and would fail in any undertaking. Not having commenced manfully to control his thoughts, he is not in a position to control affairs and to adopt serious responsibilities. He is not fit to act independently and stand alone. But he is limited, however, only by the thoughts which he chooses.

There can be no progress, no achievement, without sacrifice, and a man's worldly success will occur in the measure that he sacrifices his confused animal thoughts, and fixes his mind on the development of his plans, and the strengthening of his resolution and self-reliance. And the higher he lifts his thoughts, the more manly, upright, and righteous he will become, the greater will be his success, the more blessed and enduring will be his achievements.

The universe does not favor the greedy, the dishonest, the vicious, although on the surface it may sometimes appear to be so. It helps the honest, the magnanimous, the virtuous. All the great Teachers of the ages have declared this in varying forms, and to prove and know it a man must persist in making himself more and more virtuous by lifting up his thoughts.

## You Rise or Fall by Your Thoughts

Intellectual achievements are the result of thought concentrated to the search for knowledge, or for the beautiful and true in life or nature. Such achievements may be sometimes connected with vanity and ambition, but they are not the outcome of those characteristics; they are the natural outgrowth of long and arduous effort, and pure and unselfish thoughts.

Spiritual achievements are the consummation of holy aspirations. He who lives constantly in the conception of noble and lofty thoughts, who dwells upon all that is pure and unselfish, will, as surely as the sun reaches its zenith and the moon its full, become wise and noble in character, and rise into a position of influence and blessedness.

Achievement, of whatever kind, is the crown of effort, the diadem of thought. By the aid of self-control, resolution, purity, righteousness, and well-directed thought a man ascends; by the aid of animality, indolence, impurity, corruption, and confusion of thought a man descends.

A man may rise to high success in the world, and even to lofty altitudes in the spiritual realm, and again descend into weakness and wretchedness by allowing arrogant, selfish, and corrupt thoughts to take possession of him.

Victories attained by right thought can only be maintained by watchfulness. Many give way when success is assured, and rapidly fall back into failure.

All achievements, whether in the business, intellectual, or spiritual world, are the result of definitely directed thought, are governed by the same law, and are of the same method; the only difference lies in *the object of attainment.*

He who would accomplish little must sacrifice little; he who would achieve much must sacrifice much; he who would attain highly must sacrifice greatly.

# Visions and Ideals

THE DREAMERS ARE ARE THE SAVIORS of the world. As the visible world is sustained by the invisible, so men, through all their trials and sins and sordid vocations, are nourished by the beautiful visions  of their solitary dreamers. Humanity cannot forget its dreamers; it cannot let their ideals fade and die; it lives in them; it knows them as the realities which it shall one day see and know.

Composer, sculptor, painter, poet, prophet, sage, these are the makers of the afterworld, the architects of heaven. The world is beautiful because they have lived; without them, laboring humanity would perish.

He who cherishes a beautiful vision, a lofty ideal in his heart, will one day realize it. Columbus cherished a vision of another world, and he discovered it; Copernicus fostered the vision of a multiplicity of worlds, and he revealed it; Buddha beheld the vision of a spiritual world of stainless beauty and perfect peace, and he entered into it.

Cherish your visions; cherish your ideals; cherish the music that stirs in your heart, the beauty that forms in your mind, the loveliness that drapes your purest thoughts for out of them will grow all delightful conditions, all heavenly environment; of these, if you but remain true to them, your world will at last be built.

To desire is to obtain; to aspire is to achieve. Shall man's basest desires receive the fullest measure of gratification, and his purest aspirations starve for lack of sustenance? Such is not the law; such a condition can never be.

Dream lofty dreams, and as you dream, so shall you become. Your Vision is the promise of what you one day shall be; your Ideal is the prophecy of what you shall at last unveil.

## Dreams Beget Realities

The greatest achievement was at first and for a time a dream. The oak sleeps in the acorn; the bird waits in the egg; and in the highest vision of the soul a waking angel stirs. Dreams are the seedlings of realities.

Your circumstances may be uncongenial, but they shall not long remain so if you but perceive an Ideal and strive to reach it. You cannot travel *within* and stand still *without*.

Here is a youth hard pressed by poverty and labor; confined long hours in an unhealthy workshop; unschooled, and lacking all the arts of refinement. But he dreams of better things. He thinks of intelligence, of refinement, of grace and beauty. He conceives of, mentally builds up, an ideal condition of life; the vision of a wider liberty and a larger scope takes possession of him. Unrest urges him to action, and he utilizes all his spare time, small though they are, to the development of his latent powers and resources.

Very soon so altered has his mind become that the workshop can no longer hold him. It has become so out of harmony with his mentality that it falls out of his life as a garment is cast aside, and, with the growth of opportunities which fit the scope of his expanding powers, he passes out of it forever.

Years later we see this youth as a full-grown man. We find him a master of certain forces of the mind which he wields with world-wide influence and almost unequaled power. In his hands he holds the cords of gigantic responsibilities. He speaks, and lo! lives are changed; men and women hang upon his words and thoughts and remold their characters, and, sunlike, he becomes the fixed and luminous center around which innumerable destinies revolve. He has realized the Vision of his youth. He has become one with his Ideal.

And you, too, will realize the vision (not the idle wish) of your heart, be it base or beautiful, or a mixture of both, for you will always gravitate toward that which you, secretly, most love. In your hands will be placed the exact results of your own thoughts; you will receive that which you earn; no more, no less. Whatever your present environment may be, you will fall, remain, or rise with your thoughts, your Vision, your Ideal. You will become as small as your controlling desire; as great as your dominant aspiration.

## When the Student is Ready, The Master Will Appear

In the beautiful words of Stanton Kirkham Davis, "You may be keeping accounts, and presently you shall walk out the door that for so long seemed to you the barrier of your ideals, and you shall find yourself before an audience—the pen still behind your ear, the ink stains on your fingers—and then and there shall pour out the torrent of your inspiration.

"You may be driving sheep, and you shall wander to the city—naive and openmouthed; and under the bold guidance of the spirit wander into the studio of the master, and after a time he shall say, 'I have nothing more to teach you.' And now you have become a master, who did so recently dream of great things while driving sheep. You shall lay down the staff to take upon yourself the regeneration of the world."

### There is No Such Thing as Luck

The thoughtless, the ignorant, and the indolent, seeing only the apparent effects of things and not the things themselves, talk of luck, of fortune, and chance. Seeing a man grow rich, they say, "How lucky he is!" Observing another become intellectual, they exclaim, "How highly favored he is!" And noting the saintly character and wide influence of another, they remark, "How chance aids him at every turn!"

They do not see the trials and failures and struggles which these men have voluntarily encountered in order to gain their experience. They have no knowledge of the sacrifices these men have made, of the undaunted efforts they have put forth, of the faith they have exercised, that they might overcome the apparently insurmountable, and realize the Vision of their heart.

They do not know the darkness and the heartaches; they only see the light and joy, and call it "luck"; do not see the long and arduous journey, but only behold the pleasant goal, and call it "good fortune"; do not understand the process, but only perceive the result, and call it "chance."

In all human affairs there are *efforts*, and there are *results*, and the strength of the effort is the measure of the result. Chance is not. Gifts, powers, material, intellectual, and spiritual possessions, are the fruits of effort; they are thoughts completed, objects accomplished, visions realized.

The Vision that you glorify in your mind, the Ideal that you enthrone in your heart—this you will build your life by, this you will become.

# Serenity

CALMNESS OF MIND is one of the beautiful jewels of wisdom. It is the result of long and patient effort in self-control. Its presence is an indication of ripened experience, and of a more-than-ordinary knowledge of the laws and operations of thought.

A man becomes calm in the measure that he understands himself as a thought-evolved being for such knowledge necessitates the understanding of others as the result of thought. And as he develops a right understanding, and sees more and more clearly the internal relations of things by the action of cause and effect, he ceases to fuss and fume and worry and grieve, and remains poised, steadfast, serene.

The calm man, having learned how to govern himself, knows how to adapt himself to others; and they, in turn, revere his spiritual strength, and feel that they can learn of him and rely upon him. The more tranquil a man becomes, the greater is his success, his influence, his power for good. Even the ordinary businessman will find his business prosperity increase as he develops a greater self-control and equanimity for people always prefer to deal with a man whose behavior is strongly serene.

The strong, calm man is always loved and revered. He is like a shade-giving tree in a thirsty land, or a sheltering rock in a storm. Who does not love a tranquil heart, a sweet-tempered, balanced life? It does not matter whether it rains or shines, or what changes come to those possessing these blessings, for they are always sweet, serene, calm.

The exquisite poise of character which we call serenity is the last lesson of culture; it is the flowering of life, the fruitage of the soul. It is precious as wisdom, more to be desired than gold—yea, than even fine gold. How insignificant money-seeking looks in comparison with a serene life—a life that dwells in the ocean of Truth, beneath the waves, beyond the reach of tempests, in the Eternal Calm!

### Contentment is an Art

How many people we know who sour their lives,

who ruin all that is sweet and beautiful by explosive tempers, who destroy their poise of character, and make bad blood! It is a question of whether or not the great majority of people do not ruin their lives and mar their happiness by lack of self-control. How few people we meet in life who are well-balanced, who have that exquisite poise which is characteristic of the finished character!

Yes, humanity surges with uncontrolled passion, is tumultuous with ungoverned grief, is blown about by anxiety and doubt. Only the wise man, only he whose thoughts are controlled and purified, makes the winds and storms of the soul obey him.

Tempest-tossed souls, wherever you may be, under whatsoever conditions you may live, know this—in the ocean of life the isles of Blessedness are smiling, and the sunny shore of your ideal awaits your coming. Keep your hand firmly upon the helm of thought. In the ship of your soul reclines the commanding master; He does but sleep: wake him. Self-control is strength; Right Thought is mastery; Calmness is power. Say unto your heart, "Peace, be still!"

BOOK
TWO

# he Path to
Prosperity

# TABLE OF CONTENTS

# The Lesson of Evil

UNREST AND PAIN AND SORROW are the shadows of life. There is no heart in all the world that has not felt the sting of pain, no mind that has not been tossed upon the dark waters of trouble, no eye that has not wept the hot, blinding tears of unspeakable anguish. There is no household where the Great Destroyers, disease and death, have not entered, severing heart from heart, and casting over all the dark pall of sorrow. In the strong and apparently indestructible meshes of evil all are more or less caught fast, and pain, unhappiness and misfortune wait upon humankind.

With the object of escaping, or in some way mitigating this overshadowing gloom, men and women rush blindly into innumerable devices, pathways by which they fondly hope to enter into a happiness which will not pass away. Such are the drunkard and

the harlot, who revel in sensual excitements; such is
the exclusive aesthetic, who shuts himself out from
the sorrows of the world, and surrounds himself with
enervating luxuries; such is he who thirsts for wealth
or fame, and subordinates all things to the achievement of that object; and such are they who seek consolation in the performance of religious rites.

And to all the happiness sought seems to come,
and the soul, for a time, is lulled into a sweet security, and an intoxicating forgetfulness of the existence
of evil; but the day of disease comes at last, or some
great sorrow, temptation, or misfortune breaks suddenly in on the unfortified soul, and the fabric of its
fancied happiness is torn to shreds.

### Escaping From Pain

So over the head of every personal joy hangs the
Damoclean sword of pain, ready, at any moment, to
fall and crush the soul of him who is unprotected by
knowledge.

The child cries to be a man or woman; the man
and woman sigh for the lost felicity of childhood. The
poor person chafes under the chains of poverty by
which they are bound, and the rich often live in fear
of poverty, or scour the world in search of an elusive

shadow they call happiness.

Sometimes the soul feels that it has found a secure peace and happiness in adopting a certain religion, in embracing an intellectual philosophy, or in building up an intellectual or artistic ideal; but some overpowering temptation proves the religion to be inadequate or insufficient; the theoretical philosophy is found to be a useless prop; or in a moment, the idealistic statue upon which the devotee has for years been laboring, is shattered into fragments at his feet.

Is there, then, no way of escape from pain and sorrow? Are there no means by which the bonds of evil may be broken? Is permanent happiness, secure prosperity, and abiding peace a foolish dream?

No, there is a way, and I speak of it with gladness, by which evil can be slain forever; there is a process by which disease, poverty, or any adverse condition or circumstance can be put on one side never to return; there is a method by which a permanent prosperity can be secured, free from all fear of the return of adversity, and there is a practice by which unbroken and unending peace and bliss can be partaken of and realized. And the beginning of the way which leads to this glorious realization is *the acquirement of a right understanding of the nature of evil.*

## *Evil Must Be Understood*

It is not sufficient to deny or ignore evil; it must be understood. It is not enough to pray to God to remove the evil; you must find out why it is there, and what lesson it has for you. It is of no avail to fret and fume and chafe at the chains which bind you; you must know why and how you are bound.

Therefore, reader, you must get outside yourself, and must begin to examine and understand yourself. You must cease to be a disobedient child in the school of experience, and must begin to learn, with humility and patience, the lessons that are set for your edification and ultimate perfection; for evil, when rightly understood, is found to be, not an unlimited power or principle in the universe, but a passing phase of human experience, and it therefore becomes a teacher to those who are willing to learn.

Evil is not an abstract something outside yourself; it is an experience in your own heart, and by patiently examining and rectifying your heart you will be gradually led into the discovery of the origin and nature of evil, which will necessarily be followed by its complete eradication.

### Rooted in Ignorance

All evil is corrective and remedial, and is therefore not permanent. It is rooted in ignorance, ignorance of the true nature and relation of things, and so long as we remain in that state of ignorance, we remain subject to evil.

There is no evil in the universe which is not the result of ignorance, and which would not, if we were ready and willing to learn its lesson, lead us to higher wisdom, and then vanish away. But men remain in evil, and it does not pass away because men are not willing or prepared to learn the lesson which it came to teach them.

I knew a child who, every night when its mother took it to bed, cried to be allowed to play with the candle; and one night, when the mother was off guard for a moment, the child took hold of the candle; the inevitable result followed, and the child never wished to play with the candle again. By its one foolish act it learned perfectly the lesson of obedience, and entered into the knowledge that fire burns.

And this incident is a complete illustration of the nature, meaning and ultimate result of all sin and evil. As the child suffered through its own ignorance of the real nature of fire, so older children suffer through their ignorance of the things which they weep for and strive after, and which harm them when they are secured; the only difference being that in the latter case the ignorance and the evil are more deeply rooted and obscure.

### Darkness is Only Temporary

Evil has always been symbolized by darkness and Good by light, and hidden within the symbol is contained the perfect interpretation, the reality; for, just as light always floods the universe, and darkness is only a mere speck or shadow cast by a small body intercepting a few rays of the illimitable light, so the Light of the Supreme Good is the positive and life-giving power which floods the universe, and evil the insignificant shadow cast by the self that intercepts and shuts off the illuminating rays which strive for entrance.

When night folds the world in its black impenetrable mantle, no matter how dense the darkness, it covers but a small space of half our little planet, while the whole universe is ablaze with living light, and every soul knows that it will awake in the light of the morning.

Know, then, that when the dark night of sorrow,

pain or misfortune settles down upon your soul, and you stumble along with weary and uncertain steps, that you are merely intercepting your own personal desires between yourself and the boundless light of joy and bliss, and the dark shadow that covers you is cast by none and nothing but yourself.

And just as the darkness without is but a negative shadow, an unreality which comes from nowhere, goes to nowhere, and has no abiding dwelling-place, so the darkness within is equally a negative shadow passing over the evolving and Light-born soul.

### Learning the Lessons of Evil

"But," I fancy I hear someone say, "why pass through the darkness of evil at all?" Because, by ignorance, you have chosen to do so, and because, by doing so, you may understand both good and evil, and may the more appreciate the light by having passed through the darkness. As evil is the direct outcome of ignorance, so, when the lessons of evil are fully learned, ignorance passes away, and wisdom takes its place.

But as a disobedient child refuses to learn its lessons at school, so it is possible to refuse to learn the lessons of experience, and thus to remain in continual darkness, and to suffer continually recurring punishments in the form of disease, disappointment and sorrow. He, therefore, who would shake himself free of the evil which encompasses him, must be willing and ready to learn, and must be prepared to undergo the disciplinary process without which no grain of wisdom or abiding happiness and peace can be secured.

## Denying the Existence of Light

A person may shut themselves up in a dark room, and deny that the light exists, but it is everywhere without, and darkness exists only in his little room. So you may shut out the light of Truth, or you may begin to pull down the walls of prejudice, self-seeking and error which you have built around yourself, and so let in the glorious and omnipresent Light.

By earnest self-examination strive to realize, and not merely hold as a theory, that evil is a passing phase, a self-created shadow; that all your pains, sorrows and misfortunes have come to you by a process of undeviating and absolutely perfect law; have come to you because you deserve them and require them, and that by first enduring and then understanding them, you may be made stronger, wiser, nobler.

When you have fully entered into this realization, you will be in a position to mold your own circumstances, to transmute all evil into good, and to weave, with a master hand, the fabric of your destiny.

# The World a Reflex of Mental States

WHAT YOU ARE, SO IS YOUR WORLD. Everything in the universe is resolved into your own inward experience. It matters little what is without, for it is all a reflection of your own state of consciousness. It matters everything what you are within, for everything without will be mirrored and colored accordingly.

All that you positively know is contained in your own experience; all that you ever will know must pass through the gateway of experience, and so become part of yourself.

Your own thoughts, desires, and aspirations comprise your world, and, to you, all that there is in the universe of beauty and joy and bliss, or ugliness and sorrow and pain, is contained within yourself. By your own thoughts you make or mar your life, your world, your universe.

## Building Your World

As you build within by the power of thought, so will your outward life and circumstances shape themselves accordingly. Whatsoever you harbor in the inmost chambers of your heart will, sooner or later, by the inevitable law of reaction, shape itself in your outward life.

The soul that is impure, sordid and selfish, is gravitating with unerring precision towards misfortune and catastrophe; the soul that is pure, unselfish and noble, is gravitating with equal precision towards happiness and prosperity. Every soul attracts its own and nothing can possibly come to it that does not belong to it. To realize this is to recognize the universality of Divine Law.

The incidents of every human life, which both make and mar, are drawn to it by the quality and power of its own inner thought-life. Every soul is a complex combination of gathered experiences and thoughts, and the body is but an improvised vehicle for its manifestation. What, therefore, your thoughts are, that is your real self; and the world around, both animate and inanimate, wears the aspect with which your thoughts clothe it.

## *You Are What You Think*

"All that we are is the result of what we have thought; it is founded on our thoughts; it is made up of our thoughts." Thus said Buddha, and it therefore follows that if a person is happy, it is because they dwell in happy thoughts; if miserable, because they dwell in despondent and debilitating thoughts. Whether one be fearful or fearless, foolish or wise, troubled or serene, within that soul lies the cause of its own state or states, and never without.

And now I seem to hear a chorus of voices exclaim, "But do you really mean to say that outward circumstances do not affect our minds?" I do not say that, but I say this, and know it to be an infallible truth, that circumstances can only affect you insofar as you allow them to do so.

You are swayed by circumstances because you have not a right understanding of the nature, use, and power of thought. You believe (and upon this little word *belief* hang all our sorrows and joys) that outward things have the power to make or mar your life; by so doing you submit to those outward things, confess that you are their slave, and they your unconditional master; by so doing, you invest them with a power which they do not, of themselves, possess, and you succumb, in reality, not to the mere circumstances, but to the gloom or gladness, the fear or hope, the strength or weakness, which your thought-sphere has thrown around them.

## A Tale of Two Men

I knew two men who, at an early age, lost the hard-earned savings of years. One was very deeply troubled, and gave way to chagrin, worry, and despondency.

The other, on reading in his morning newspaper that the bank in which his money was deposited had hopelessly failed, and that he had lost all, quietly and firmly remarked, "Well, it's gone, and trouble and worry won't bring it back, but hard work will." He went to work with renewed vigor, and rapidly became prosperous, while the former man, continuing to mourn the loss of his money, and to grumble at his "bad luck," remained the sport and tool of adverse circumstances, in reality of his own weak and slavish thoughts.

The loss of money was a curse to the one because he clothed the event with dark and dreary thoughts; it was a blessing to the other, because he threw around it thoughts of strength, of hope, and renewed endeavor.

If circumstances had the power to bless or harm, they would bless and harm all men alike, but the fact that the same circumstance will be alike good and bad to different souls proves that the good or bad is not in the circumstance, but only in the mind of him that encounters it.

When you begin to realize this you will begin to control your thoughts, to regulate and discipline your mind, and to rebuild the inward temple of your soul, eliminating all useless and superfluous material, and incorporating into your being thoughts alone of joy and serenity, of strength and life, of compassion and love, of beauty and immortality; and as you do this you will become joyful and serene, strong and healthy, compassionate and loving, and beautiful with the beauty of immortality.

## One Man's Treasure is Trash to Another

And as we clothe events with the drapery of our own thoughts, so likewise do we clothe the objects of the visible world around us, and where one sees harmony and beauty, another sees revolting ugliness.

An enthusiastic naturalist was one day roaming the country lanes in pursuit of his hobby, and during his rambles came upon a pool of brackish water near a farmyard. As he proceeded to fill a small bottle with the water for purpose of examination under the microscope, he dilated, with more enthusiasm than discretion, to an uncultivated son of a farmer who stood close by, upon the hidden and innumerable wonders contained in the pool, and concluded by saying, "Yes, my friend, within this pool is contained a hundred, nay, a million universes, had we the sense or the instrument by which we could apprehend them."

And the unsophisticated one ponderously remarked, "I know the water is full of tadpoles, but they are easy to catch."

Where the naturalist, his mind stored with the knowledge of natural facts, saw beauty, harmony and hidden glory, the mind unenlightened upon those things saw only an offensive mud-puddle.

The wildflower which the casual wayfarer thoughtlessly tramples upon is, to the spiritual eye of the poet, an angelic messenger from the invisible. To the many, the ocean is but a dreary expanse of water on which ships sail and are sometimes wrecked; to the soul of a musician it is a living thing, and he hears, in all its changing moods, divine harmonies.

Where the ordinary mind sees disaster and confusion, the mind of the philosopher sees the perfect sequence of cause and effect, and where the materialist sees nothing but endless death, the mystic sees pulsating and eternal life.

## *Making Judgement of Others*

And as we clothe both events and objects with our own thoughts, so likewise do we clothe the souls of others in the garments of our thoughts.

The suspicious believe everybody to be suspicious; the liar feels secure in the thought that he is not so foolish as to believe that there is such a phenomenon as a strictly truthful person; the envious see envy in every soul; the miser thinks everybody is eager to get his money; he who has subordinated conscience in the making of his wealth, sleeps with a revolver under his pillow, rapt in the delusion that the world is filled with conscienceless people who are eager to rob him, and the abandoned sensualist looks upon the saint as a hypocrite.

On the other hand, those who dwell in loving thoughts, see that in all which calls forth their love and sympathy; the trusting and honest are not troubled by suspicions; the good-natured and charitable who rejoice at the good fortune of others, scarcely know what envy means; and he who has realized the Divine within himself recognizes it in all beings, even in the beasts.

And men and women are confirmed in their mental outlook because of the fact that, by the law of cause and effect, they attract to themselves that which they send forth, and so come in contact with people similar to themselves. The old adage, "Birds of a feather flock together," has a deeper significance than is generally attached to it, for in the thought-world as in the world of matter, each clings to its kind.

> *Do you wish for kindness? Be kind.*
> *Do you ask for truth? Be true.*
> *What you give of yourself you find;*
> *Your world is a reflex of you.*

### The Kingdom of God is Within

If you are one of those who are praying for, and looking forward to, a happier world beyond the grave, here is a message of gladness for you: you may enter into and realize that happy world now; it fills the whole universe, and is within you, waiting for you to find, acknowledge, and possess.

Said one who knew the inner laws of Being, "When men shall say lo here, or lo there, do not go after them; the kingdom of God is within you."

What you have to do is to believe this, simply believe it with a mind unshadowed by doubt, and then meditate upon it till you understand it. You will then begin to purify and to build your inner world, and as you proceed, passing from revelation to revelation, from realization to realization, you will discover the utter powerlessness of outward things beside the magic potency of a self-governed soul.

*If thou wouldest right the world,*
*And banish all the evils and its woes,*
*Make its wild places bloom,*
*And its drear deserts blossom as the rose,—*
*Then right thyself.*

*If thou wouldest turn the world*
*From its long captivity in sin,*
*Restore all broken hearts,*
*Slay grief, and let sweet consolation in,—*
*Turn thou thyself.*

*If thou wouldest cure the world*

Of its long sickness, end its grief and pain;
Bring in all-healing Joy,
And give to the afflicted rest again,—
Then cure thyself.

If thou wouldest wake the world
Out of its dream of death and darkening strife
Bring it to Love and Peace,
And Light and brightness of immortal Life,—
Wake thou thyself.

# The Way Out of Undesirable Conditions

**H**AVING SEEN AND REALIZED that evil is but a passing shadow thrown, by the intercepting self, across the transcendent Form of the Eternal Good, and that the world is a mirror in which each sees a reflection of himself or herself, we now ascend, by firm easy steps, to that plane of perception whereon is seen and realized the Vision of the Law.

With this realization comes the knowledge that everything is included in a ceaseless interaction of cause and effect, and that nothing can possibly be divorced from law. From the most trivial thought, word, or act of man or woman, up to the groupings of the celestial bodies, law reigns supreme.

No arbitrary condition can, even for a moment, exist, for such a condition would be a denial and an annihilation of law. Every condition of life is, therefore, bound up in an orderly and harmonious sequence, and the secret and cause of every condition is contained within itself.

### The Law of Cause and Effect

The law, "Whatsoever a man sows that shall he also reap," is inscribed in flaming letters upon the portal of Eternity, and none can deny it, none can cheat it, none can escape it. He who puts his hand in the fire must suffer the burning until such time as it has worked itself out, and neither curses nor prayers can avail to alter it. And precisely the same law governs the realm of mind.

Hatred, anger, jealousy, envy, lust, covetousness, all these are fires which burn, and whoever even so much as touches them must suffer the torments of burning. All these conditions of mind are rightfully called "evil" for they are the efforts of the soul to subvert, in its ignorance, the law, and they therefore lead to chaos and confusion within, and are sooner or later actualized in the outward circumstances as disease, failure, and misfortune, coupled with grief, pain and despair.

Whereas love, gentleness, goodwill, purity, are cooling airs which breathe peace upon the soul that woos them, and, being in harmony with the Eternal Law, they become actualized in the form of health, peaceful surroundings, and undeviating success and good fortune.

## Obedience To the Law

A thorough understanding of this Great Law which permeates the universe leads to the acquiring of that state of mind know as *obedience*. To know that justice, harmony, and love are supreme in the universe is likewise to know that all adverse and painful conditions are the result of our own disobedience to that Law. Such knowledge leads to strength and power, and it is upon such knowledge alone that a true life and an enduring success and happiness can be built.

To be patient under all circumstances, and to accept all conditions as necessary factors in your training, is to rise superior to all painful conditions, and to overcome them with an overcoming which is sure, and which leaves no fear of their return, for by the power of obedience to law, they are utterly slain. Such an obedient one is working in harmony with the law, has, in fact, identified himself with the law, and whatsoever he conquers he conquers forever; whatsoever he builds cannot be destroyed.

## Life is What You Make of It

The cause of all power, as of all weakness, is within: the secret of all happiness as of all misery is likewise within. There is no progress apart from unfoldment within, and no sure foothold of prosperity or peace except by orderly advancement of knowledge.

You say you are chained by circumstances; you cry out for better opportunities, for a wider scope, for improved physical conditions, and perhaps you inwardly curse the fate that binds you hand and foot. It is for you that I write; it is to you that I speak. Listen, and let my words burn themselves into your heart, for that which I say to you is truth: *You may bring about that improved condition in your outward life which you desire, if you will unswervingly resolve to improve your inner life.*

I know this pathway looks barren at its commencement (truth always does; it is only error and delusion which are at first inviting and fascinating), but if you undertake to walk it; if you perseveringly discipline your mind, eradicating your weaknesses, and allowing your soul-forces and spiritual powers to unfold themselves, you will be astonished at the magical changes which will be brought about in your outward life.

As you proceed, golden opportunities will be strewn across your path, and the power and judgement to properly utilize them will spring up within you. Genial friends will come unbidden to you; sympathetic souls will be drawn to you as the needle is to the magnet; and books and all outward aids that you require will come unsought.

## Stop Complaining

Perhaps the chains of poverty hang heavily upon you, and you are friendless and alone, and you long with an intense longing that your load may be lightened; but the load continues, and you seem to be enveloped in an ever-increasing darkness. Perhaps you complain, you bewail your lot; you blame your birth, your parents, your employer, or the unjust Powers who have bestowed upon you so undeservedly poverty and hardship, and upon another affluence and ease.

Cease your complaining and fretting; none of these things which you blame are the cause of your poverty; the cause is within yourself, and where the cause is, there is the remedy. The very fact that you are a complainer shows that you deserve your lot, shows that you lack faith which is the ground of all effort and progress.

There is no room for a complainer in a universe of law, and worry is soul-suicide. By your very attitude of mind you are strengthening the chains which bind you, and are drawing about you the darkness by which you are enveloped.

Alter your outlook upon life, and your outward life will alter. Build yourself up in faith and knowledge, and make yourself worthy of better surroundings and wider opportunities. Be sure, first of all, that you are making the best of what you have. Do not delude yourself into supposing that you can step into greater advantages while overlooking smaller ones, for if you could, the advantage would be impermanent and you would quickly fall back again in order to learn the lesson which you had neglected.

As the child at school must master one lesson before passing on to the next, so, before you can have the greater good which you so desire, must you faithfully employ that which you already possess. The Biblical parable of the talents is a beautiful story illustrative of this truth, for does it not plainly show that if we misuse, neglect, or degrade that which we possess, be it ever so mean and insignificant, even that little will be taken from us, for, by our conduct we show that we are unworthy of it.

### Ennoble Your Surroundings

Perhaps you are living in a small cottage, and are surrounded by unhealthy and malicious influences. You desire a larger and more sanitary residence. Then you must fit yourself for such a residence by first of all making your cottage as far as possible a little paradise.

Keep it spotlessly clean. Make it look as pretty and sweet as your limited means will allow. Cook your plain food with all care, and arrange your humble table as tastefully as you possibly can. If you cannot afford a carpet, let your rooms be carpeted with smiles and welcomes, fastened down with the nails of kind words driven in with the hammer of patience. Such a carpet will not fade in the sun and constant use will never wear it away.

By so ennobling your present surroundings you will rise above them, and above the need of them, and at the right time you will pass on into the better house and surroundings which have all along been waiting for you, and which you have fitted yourself to occupy.

Perhaps you desire more time for thought and effort, and feel your hours of labor are too hard and long. Then see to it that you are utilizing to the fullest possible extent what little spare time you have. It is useless to desire more time, if you are already wasting what little time you have, for you would only grow more indolent and indifferent.

## Evils Are Blessings in Disguise

Even poverty and lack of time and leisure are not the evils that you imagine they are, and if they hinder you in your progress, it is because you have clothed them in your own weaknesses, and the evil that you see in them is really in yourself.

Endeavor to fully and completely realize that insofar as you shape and mold your mind, you are the maker of your destiny, and as, by the transmuting power of self-discipline you realize this more and more, you will come to see that these so-called evils may be converted into blessings.

You will then utilize your poverty for the cultivation of patience, hope and courage, and your lack of time in the gaining of promptness of action and decision of mind, by seizing the precious moments as they present themselves for your acceptance.

As in the rankest soil the most beautiful flowers are grown, so in the dark soil of poverty the choicest flowers of humanity have developed and bloomed.

Where there are difficulties to cope with, and unsatisfactory conditions to overcome, there virtue most flourishes and manifests its glory.

It may be that you are in the employ of a tyrannous master or mistress, and you feel that you are harshly treated. Look upon this also as necessary to your training. Return your employer's unkindness with gentleness and forgiveness. Practice unceasingly patience and self-control. Turn the disadvantage to account by utilizing it for the gaining of mental and spiritual strength, and by your silent example and influence you will thus be teaching your employer, will be helping him to grow ashamed of his conduct, and will, at the same time, be lifting yourself up to the height of spiritual attainment by which you will be enabled to step into new and more congenial surroundings at the time when they are presented to you.

## Cease Being a Slave

Do not complain that you are a slave, but lift yourself up, by noble conduct, above the plane of slavery. Before complaining that you are a slave to another, be sure that you are not a slave to self.

Look within; look searchingly, and have no mercy

upon yourself. You will find there, perchance, slavish thoughts, slavish desires, and in your daily life and conduct slavish habits. Conquer these; cease to be a slave to self, and no person will have the power to enslave you. As you overcome self, you will overcome all adverse conditions, and every difficulty will fall before you.

Do not complain that you are oppressed by the rich. Are you sure that if you gained riches you would not be an oppressor yourself? Remember that there is the Eternal Law which is absolutely just, and that he who oppresses today must himself be oppressed tomorrow; and from this there is no escape. And perhaps you, yesterday (in some former existence) were rich and an oppressor, and you are now merely paying off the debt which you owe the Great Law. Practice, therefore, fortitude and faith. Dwell constantly in mind upon the Eternal Justice, the Eternal Good.

Endeavor to lift yourself above the personal and the transitory into the impersonal and permanent. Shake off the delusion that you are being injured or oppressed by another, and try to realize, by a profounder comprehension of your inner life, that you are only really injured by what is within you.

## *The Acquisition of Virtue*

There is no practice more degrading, debasing and soul-destroying than that of *self-pity*. Cast it out from you. While such a canker is feeding upon your heart, you can never expect to grow into a fuller life. Cease from the condemnation of others, and cease to condemn yourself. Condone none of your acts, desires and thoughts that do not bear comparison with spotless purity, or endure the light of sinless good. By so doing you will be building your house upon a rock of the Eternal, and all that is required for your happiness and well-being will come to you in its own time.

There is positively no way of permanently rising above poverty, or any undesirable condition, except by eradicating those selfish and negative conditions within, of which these are the reflection, and by virtue of which they continue. The way to true riches is to enrich the soul by the acquisition of virtue. Outside of real heart-virtue there is neither prosperity nor power, but only the appearances of these.

I am aware that men make money who have acquired no measure of virtue, and have little desire to do so; but such money does not constitute true riches, and its possession is transitory and feverish.

Here is David's testimony: "For I was envious at the foolish when I saw the prosperity of the wicked... Their eyes stand out with fatness; they have more than the heart could wish... Verily I have cleansed my heart in vain, and washed my hands in innocence... When I thought to know this it was too painful for me, until I went into the sanctuary of God; then understood I their end."

## *Riches Are Barren of Virtue*

The prosperity of the wicked was a great trial to David until he went into the sanctuary of God, and then he *knew their end.* You likewise may go into that sanctuary. It is within you. It is that state of consciousness which remains when all that is sordid, and personal, and impermanent is risen above, and universal and eternal principles are realized. That is the God state of consciousness; it is the sanctuary of the Most High.

When, by long strife and self-discipline, you have succeeded in entering the door of that holy Temple, you will perceive, with unobstructed vision, the end and the fruit of all human thought and endeavor, both good and evil. You will then no longer relax your faith when you see the immoral man accumulating outward riches, for you know that he must come again to poverty and degradation.

The rich man who is barren of virtue is, in reality, poor, and as surely as the waters of the river are drifting to the ocean, so surely is he, in the midst of all his riches, drifting towards poverty and misfortune; and though he die rich, yet must he return to reap the bitter fruit of all his immorality. And though he become rich many times, yet as many times he must be thrown back into poverty, until, by long experience and suffering he conquers the poverty within.

But the man who is outwardly poor, yet rich in virtue, is truly rich, and, in the midst of his poverty, he is surely traveling towards prosperity; and abounding joy and bliss await his coming.

If you would become truly and permanently prosperous, you must first become virtuous. It is therefore unwise to aim directly at prosperity, to make it the one object of life, to reach out greedily for it. To do this is to ultimately defeat yourself. But rather aim at self-perfection, make useful and unselfish service the object of your life, and ever reach out hands of faith towards the supreme and unalterable Good.

### *Scrutinize Your Motives*

You say you desire wealth, not for your own sake, but in order to do good with it, and to bless others. If this is your real motive in desiring wealth, then wealth will come to you; for you are strong and unselfish indeed if, in the midst of riches, you are willing to look upon yourself as steward and not as owner.

But examine well your motive, for in the majority of instances where money is desired for the admitted object of blessing others, the real underlying motive is a love of popularity, and a desire to pose as a philanthropist or reformer.

If you are not doing good with what little you have, depend upon it—the more money you got the more selfish you would become, and all the good you appeared to do with your money, if you attempted to do any, would be so much insinuating self-praise.

If your real desire is to do good, there is no need to wait for money before you do it; you can do it now, this very moment, and just where you are. If you are really so unselfish as you believe yourself to be, you will show it by sacrificing yourself for others now. No matter how poor you are, there is room for self-sacrifice, for did not the widow put her all into the treasury?

The heart that truly desires to do good does not wait for money before doing it, but comes to the altar of sacrifice, and, leaving there the unworthy elements of self, goes out and breathes upon neighbor and stranger, friend and enemy alike, the breath of blessedness.

As the effect is related to the cause, so is prosperity and power related to the inward good, and poverty and weakness to the inward evil.

### What is True Wealth?

Money does not constitute true wealth, nor position, nor power, and to rely upon it alone is to stand upon a slippery place.

Your true wealth is your stock of virtue, and your true power the uses to which you put it. Rectify your heart, and you will rectify your life. Lust, hatred, anger, vanity, pride, covetousness, self-indulgence, self-seeking, obstinacy—all these are poverty and weakness; whereas, love, purity, gentleness, meekness, patience, compassion, generosity, self-forgetfulness, and self-renunciation—all these are wealth and power.

As the elements of power and weakness are overcome, an irresistible and all-conquering power is evolved from within, and he who succeeds in establishing himself in the highest virtue, brings the whole world to his feet.

But the rich, as well as the poor, have their undesirable conditions and are frequently farther removed from happiness than the poor. And here we see how happiness depends, not upon outward aids or possessions, but upon the inward life.

Perhaps you are an employer, and you have endless troubles with those whom you employ, and when you do get good and faithful servants they quickly leave you. As a result you are beginning to lose, or have completely lost, your faith in human nature. You try to remedy matters by giving better wages, and by allowing certain liberties, yet matters remain unaltered. Let me advise you.

The secret of all your trouble is not in your servants, *it is in yourself*; and if you look within, with a humble and sincere desire to discover and eradicate your error, you will, sooner or later, find the origin of your unhappiness.

It may be some selfish desire, or lurking suspicion, or unkind attitude of mind which sends out its poison upon those about you, and reacts upon yourself, even though you may not show it in your manner or speech. Think of your workers with kindness, consider their happiness and comfort, and never demand of them that extremity of service which you yourself would not care to perform were you in their place.

Rare and beautiful is that humility of soul by which a servant entirely forgets himself in his master's good; but far rarer, and beautiful with a divine beauty, is that nobility of soul by which a man, forgetting his own happiness, seeks the happiness of those who are under his authority, and who depend upon him for their bodily sustenance. And such a man's happiness is increased tenfold, nor does he need to complain of those whom he employs.

Said a well-known and extensive employer of labor, who never needs to dismiss an employee: "I have always had the happiest relations with my workers. If you ask me how it is to be accounted for, I can only say that it has been my aim from the first to do them as I would wish to be done." Herein lies the secret by which all desirable conditions are secured, and all that are undesirable are overcome.

### The Way Out

Do you say that you are lonely and unloved, and

have "not a friend in the world"? Then, I pray you, for the sake of your own happiness, blame nobody but yourself. Be friendly towards others, and friends will soon flock round you. Make yourself pure and lovable, and you will be loved by all.

Whatever conditions are rendering your life burdensome, you may pass out of and beyond them by developing and utilizing within you the transforming power of self-purification and self-conquest. Be it that poverty which galls (and remember that the poverty upon which I have been dilating is that poverty which is a source of misery, and not that voluntary poverty which is the glory of emancipated souls), or the riches which burden, or the many misfortunes, griefs, and annoyances which form the dark background in the web of life, you may overcome them by overcoming the selfish elements within which give them life.

It matters not that by the unfailing Law there are past thoughts and acts to work out and to atone for, as, by the same law, we are setting in motion, during every moment of our life, fresh thoughts and acts, and we have the power to make them good or ill. Nor does it follow that if we (reaping what we have sown) must lose money or forfeit position, that we must also lose our fortitude or forfeit our uprightness, and it is in these that our wealth and power and happiness are to be found.

The person who clings to self is his or her own enemy, and is surrounded by enemies. The person who relinquishes self is his or her own savior, and is surrounded by friends like a protecting belt. Before the divine radiance of a pure heart all darkness vanishes and all clouds melt away, and the one who has conquered self has conquered the universe. Come, then, out of your poverty; come out of your pain; come out of your troubles, and sighings, and complainings, and heartaches, and loneliness *by coming out of yourself.*

Let the old tattered garment of your petty selfishness fall from you, and put on a new garment of universal Love. You will then realize the inward heaven, and it will be reflected in your outward life.

The person who sets their foot firmly upon the path of self-conquest, who walks, aided by the staff of Faith, the highway of self-sacrifice, will assuredly achieve the highest prosperity, and will reap abounding and enduring joy and bliss.

# The Silent Power
of Thought

THE MOST POWERFUL forces in the universe are
the silent forces; and in accordance with the
intensity of its power does a force become
beneficent when rightly directed, and destructive
when wrongly employed. This is common knowledge
in regard to the mechanical forces, such as steam,
electricity, etc., but few have yet learned to apply this
knowledge to the realm of the mind, where thought
forces (most powerful of all) are continually being
generated and sent forth as currents of salvation or
destruction.

At this stage of our evolution, humankind has
entered into the possession of these forces and the
whole trend of our present advancement is their
complete subjugation. All the wisdom possible to
man and woman on this material earth is to be found
only in complete self-mastery, and the command,

"Love your enemies," resolves itself into an exhortation to enter, here and now, into the possession of that sublime wisdom by taking hold of, mastering and transmuting, those mind forces to which people are now slavishly subject, and by which they are helplessly borne, like a straw on the stream, upon the currents of selfishness.

The Hebrew prophets, with their perfect knowledge of the Supreme Law, always related outward events to inward thought, and associated national disaster or success with the thoughts and desires that dominated the nation at the time. The knowledge of the causal power of thought is the basis of all their prophecies, as it is the basis of all real wisdom and power.

National events are simply the working out of the psychic forces of the nation. Wars, plagues, and famines are the meeting and clashing of wrongly-directed thought-forces, the culminating points at which destruction steps in as the agent of the Law. It is foolish to ascribe war to the influence of one person, or to one body of people. It is the crowning horror of national selfishness.

## Matter is Objectified Thought

It is the silent and conquering thought-forces which bring all things into manifestation. The universe grew out of thought. Matter in its last analysis is found to be merely objectified thought. All of humankind's accomplishments were first wrought out in thought, and then objectified. The author, the inventor, the architect, first builds up their work in thought, and having perfected it in all its parts as a complete and harmonious whole upon the thought-plane, then commence to materialize it, to bring it down to the material or sense-plane.

When the thought-forces are directly in harmony with the overruling Law, they are uplifting and preservative, but when subverted they become disintegrating and self-destructive.

To adjust all your thoughts to a perfect and unswerving faith in the omnipotence and supremacy of Good, is to cooperate with that Good, and to realize within yourself the solution and destruction of all evil. *Believe and ye shall live*. And here we have the true meaning of salvation; salvation from the darkness and negation of evil, by entering into, and realizing the living light of the Eternal Good.

## Overcoming Negative Thoughts

Where there is fear, worry, anxiety, doubt, trouble, chagrin, or disappointment, there is ignorance and lack of faith.

All these conditions of mind are the direct outcome of selfishness, and are based upon an inherent belief in the power and supremacy of evil; they therefore constitute practical atheism; and to live in, and become subject to, these negative and soul-destroying conditions of the mind is the only real atheism.

It is salvation from such conditions that the race needs, and let no man or woman boast of salvation while they are their helpless and obedient slave. To fear or to worry is as sinful as to curse, for how can one fear or worry if they intrinsically believe in Eternal Justice, the Omnipotent Good, the Boundless Love? To fear, to worry, to doubt, is to deny, to disbelieve.

It is from such states of mind that all weakness and failure proceed, for they represent the annulling and disintegrating of the positive thought-forces which would otherwise speed to their object with power, and bring about their own beneficent results.

To overcome these negative conditions is to enter into a life of power, is to cease to be a slave, and to become a master, and there is only one way by which they can be overcome, and that is by *steady and persistent growth in inward knowledge.*

To mentally deny evil is not sufficient; it must, by daily practice, be risen above and understood. To mentally affirm the good is inadequate; it must, by unswerving endeavor, be entered into and comprehended.

The intelligent practice of self-control quickly leads to a knowledge of one's interior thought-forces and, later on, to the acquisition of that power by which they are rightly employed and directed. In the measure that you master self, that you control your mental forces instead of being controlled by them, in just such measure will you master affairs and outward circumstances.

## Being a Slave to Circumstances

Show me a person under whose touch everything crumbles away, and who cannot retain success even when it is placed in their hands, and I will show you a person who dwells continually in those conditions of mind which are the very negation of power.

To be forever wallowing in the bogs of doubt, to be drawn continuously into the quicksand of fear, or blown ceaselessly about by the winds of anxiety, is to be a slave, and to live the life of a slave, even though success and influence be forever knocking at your door seeking for admittance. Such a person, being without faith and without self-government, is incapable of the right government of their affairs, and is a slave to circumstances; in reality a slave to themselves. Such are taught by affliction, and ultimately pass from weakness to strength by the stress of bitter experience.

## Disciplining Your Mind

Faith and purpose constitute the motive-power of life. There is nothing that a strong faith and an unflinching purpose may not accomplish. By the daily exercise of simple faith, the thought-forces are gathered together, and by the daily strengthening of silent purpose, those forces are directed towards the object of accomplishment.

Whatever your position in life may be, before you can hope to enter into any measure of success, usefulness, and power, you must learn how to focus your thought-forces by cultivating calm and repose. It may be that you are a business person, and you are suddenly confronted with some overwhelming difficulty or probable disaster. You grow fearful and anxious, and are at your wit's end. To persist in such a state of mind would be fatal, for when anxiety steps in, correct judgement passes out.

Now if you will take advantage of a quiet hour or two in the early morning or at night, and go away to some solitary spot, or to some room in your house where you know you will be absolutely free from intrusion, you forcibly direct your mind right away from the object of anxiety by dwelling upon something in your life that is pleasing and bliss-giving, a calm reposeful strength will gradually steal into your mind, and your anxiety will pass away.

Upon the instant that you find your mind reverting to the lower plane of worry bring it back again, and reestablish it on the plane of peace and strength. When this is fully accomplished, you may then concentrate your whole mind upon the solution of your difficulty, and what was intricate and insurmountable to you in your hour of anxiety will be made plain and easy, and you will see, with that clear vision and perfect judgement which belong only to a calm and untroubled mind, the right course to pursue and the proper end to be brought about.

### Calming the Mind

It may be that you will have to try day after day

before you will be able to perfectly calm your mind, but if you persevere, you will certainly accomplish it. And the course which is presented to you in that hour of calmness *must be carried out*.

Doubtless when you are again involved in the business of the day, and worries again creep in and begin to dominate you, you will begin to think that the course is a wrong or foolish one, but do not heed such suggestions. Be guided absolutely and entirely by the vision of calmness, and not by the shadows of anxiety.

The hour of calmness is the hour of illumination and correct judgement. By such a course of mental discipline the scattered thought-forces are reunited, and directed, like the rays of the searchlight, upon the problem at issue, with the result that it gives way before them.

There is no difficulty, however great, that will not yield before a calm and powerful concentration of thought, and no legitimate object that will not be speedily actualized by the intelligent use and direction of one's soul-forces.

Not until you have gone deeply and searchingly into your inner nature, and have overcome many enemies that lurk there, can you have any approximate conception of the subtle power of thought, of its inseparable relation to outward and material things, or of its magical potency, when rightly poised and directed, in readjusting and transforming the conditions of life.

### Thoughts Are Forces

Every thought you think is a force sent out, and in accordance with its nature and intensity will it go out to seek lodging in minds receptive to it, and will react upon yourself for good or evil. There is ceaseless reciprocity between mind and mind, and a continual interchange of thought-forces.

Selfish and disturbing thoughts are so many malignant and destructive forces, messengers of evil, sent out to stimulate and augment the evil in other minds, which in turn send them back upon you with added power.

While thoughts that are calm, pure and unselfish are so many angelic messengers sent out into the world with health, healing, and blessedness upon their wings, counteracting the evil forces; pouring the oil of joy upon the troubled waters of anxiety and sorrow, and restoring to broken hearts their heritage of immortality.

Think good thoughts, and they will quickly become actualized in your outward life in the form of good conditions. Control your soul-forces, and you will be able to shape your outward life as you will. The difference between a savior and a sinner is this: that the one has a perfect control of all the forces within him; the other is dominated and controlled by them.

## Going into the Silence

There is absolutely no other way to true power and abiding peace, but by self-control, self-government, self-purification. To be at the mercy of your disposition is to be impotent, unhappy, and of little real use in the world. The conquest of your petty likes and dislikes, your capricious loves and hates, your fits of anger, suspicion, jealousy, and all the changing moods to which you are more or less helplessly subject, this is the task you have before you if you would weave into the web of life the golden threads of happiness and prosperity.

Insofar as you are enslaved by the changing moods within you, will you need to depend upon others and upon outward aids as you walk through life. If you would walk firmly and securely, and would accomplish any achievement, you must learn to rise above and control all such disturbing and retarding vibrations.

You must daily practice the habit of putting your mind at rest, "going into the silence" as it is commonly called. This is the method of replacing a troubled thought with one of peace, a thought of weakness with one of strength. Until you succeed in doing this you cannot hope to direct your mental forces upon the problems and pursuits of life with any appreciable measure of success.

It is a process of diverting one's scattered forces into one powerful channel. Just as a useless marsh may be converted into a field of golden corn or a fruitful garden by draining and directing the scattered and harmful streams into one well-cut channel, so, he who acquires calmness, and subdues and directs the thought currents within himself, saves his soul, and fructifies his heart and life.

### The Power of Self-Mastery

As you succeed in gaining mastery over your impulses and thoughts you will begin to feel, growing up within you, a new and silent power, and a settled feeling of composure and strength will remain with you. Your latent powers will begin to unfold themselves, and whereas formerly your efforts were weak and ineffectual, you will now be able to work with that calm confidence which commands success.

And along with this new power and strength, there will be awakened within you that interior illumination known as "intuition," and you will walk no longer in darkness and speculation, but in light and certainty.

With the development of this soul-vision, judgement and mental penetration will be incalculably increased, and there will evolve within you that prophetic vision by the aid of which you will be able to sense coming events, and to forecast, with remarkable accuracy, the result of your efforts.

And in just the measure that you alter from within will your outlook upon life alter; and as you alter your mental attitude towards others they will alter in their attitude and conduct towards you. As you rise above the lower, debilitating, and destructive thought-forces, you will come into contact with the positive, strengthening, and up-building currents generated by strong, pure, and noble minds, your happiness will be immeasurably intensified, and you will begin to realize the joy, strength, and power, which are only born of self-mastery.

And this joy, strength, and power will be continually radiating from you, and without any effort on your part, nay, though you are utterly unconscious of it, strong people will be drawn towards you, influence will be put into your hands, and in accordance with your altered thought-world will outward events shape themselves.

"One's foes are they of our own household," and they who would be useful, strong, and happy, must cease to be passive receptacles for the negative, beggarly, and impure streams of thought; and as a wise householder commands servants and invites guests, so must we learn to command our desires, and to say, with authority, what thoughts we shall admit into the mansion of our soul. Even a very partial success in self-mastery adds greatly to one's power, and those who succeed in perfecting this divine accomplishment, enter into the possession of undreamed-of wisdom and inward strength and peace, and realize that all the forces of the universe aid and protect their footsteps who is master of his soul.

# The Secret of
# Health, Success, & Power

We all remember with what delight, as children, we listened to the never-tiring fairy tale. How eagerly we followed the fluctuating fortunes of the good boy or girl, ever protected in the hour of crisis, from the evil machinations of the scheming witch, the cruel giant, or the wicked hag. And our little hearts never faltered for the fate of the hero or heroine, nor did we doubt their ultimate triumph over all their enemies, for we knew that the fairies were infallible, and they would never desert those who had concentrated themselves to the good and the true.

And what unspeakable joy pulsated within us when the Fairy-Queen, bringing all her magic to bear at the critical moment, scattered all the darkness and trouble, and granted them the complete satisfaction of all their hopes, and they were "happy ever after."

With the accumulating years, and an ever-increasing intimacy with the so-called "realities" of life, our beautiful fairy-world became obliterated, and its wonderful inhabitants were relegated, in the archives of memory, to the shadowy and unreal. And we thought we were wise and strong in thus leaving forever the land of childish dreams, but as we re-become little children in the wondrous world of wisdom, we shall return again to the inspiring dreams of childhood and find that they are, after all, realities.

The fairy-folk, so small and nearly always invisible, yet possessed of an all-conquering and magical power, who bestow upon the good, health, wealth and happiness, along with the gifts of nature in lavish profusion, start again into reality and become immortalized in the soul-realm of him who, by growth in wisdom, has entered into knowledge of the power of thought, and the laws which govern the inner world of being. To him, the fairies live again as thought-people, thought-messengers, thought-powers in working harmony with the over-ruling Good. And they who, day by day, endeavor to harmonize their hearts with the heart of the Supreme Good, do in reality acquire true health, wealth, and happiness.

## *The Power of Goodness*

There is no protection to compare with goodness, and by "goodness" I do not mean a mere outward conformity to the rules of morality; I mean pure thought, noble inspiration, unselfish love, and freedom from vainglory. To dwell continually in good thoughts is to throw around oneself a psychic atmosphere of sweetness and power which leaves its impress upon all who come in contact with it.

As the rising sun puts to rout the helpless shadows, so are all the impotent forces of evil put to flight by the searching rays of positive thought which shine forth from a heart made strong in purity and faith.

Where there is sterling faith and uncompromising purity there is health, there is success, there is power. In such a one, disease, failure, and disaster can find no lodging, for there is nothing on which they can feed.

## *Disease Begins in the Mind*

Even physical conditions are largely determined by mental states, and to this truth the scientific world is rapidly being drawn. The old, materialistic belief that we are what our body makes us, is rapidly passing away, and is being replaced by the inspiring belief that we are superior to our body, and that our body is what we make it by the power of thought. People everywhere are ceasing to believe that a person is despairing because they are ill, and are coming to understand that they are ill because they are despairing, and in the near future, the fact that all disease has its origin in the mind will become common knowledge.

There is no evil in the universe but has its root and origin in the mind, and sin, sickness, sorrow and affliction do not, in reality, belong to the universal order, are not inherent in the nature of things, but are the direct outcome of our ignorance of the right relations of things.

According to tradition, there once lived, in India, a school of philosophers who led a life of such absolute purity and simplicity that they commonly reached the age of one hundred and fifty years, and to fall sick was looked upon by them as an unpardonable disgrace, for it was considered to indicate a violation of law.

The sooner we realize and acknowledge that sickness, far from being the arbitrary visitation of an offended God, or the test of an unwise Providence, is the result of our own error or sin, the sooner shall we enter upon the highway of health. Disease comes to those who attract it, to those whose minds and bodies are receptive to it, and flees from those whose strong, pure, and positive thought-sphere generates healing and life-giving currents.

### Negative Emotions = Sickness

If you are given to anger, worry, jealousy, greed, or any other inharmonious state of mind, and expect perfect physical health, you are expecting the impossible, for you are continually sowing the seeds of disease in your mind. Such conditions of mind are carefully shunned by the wise one, for he or she knows them to be far more dangerous than a bad drain or an infected house.

If you would be free from all physical aches and pains, and would enjoy perfect physical harmony, then put your mind in order, and harmonize your thoughts. Think joyful thoughts; think loving thoughts; allow the elixir of goodwill to flow through your veins and you will need no other medicine.

Put away your jealousies, your suspicions, your worries, your hatreds, your self indulgences, and you will put away your illness, your fatigue, your nervousness and aching joints. If you will persist in clinging to these debilitating and demoralizing habits of mind, then do not complain when your body is laid low with sickness.

The following story illustrates the close relationship between habits of the mind and bodily conditions: A certain man was afflicted with a painful disease, and he tried one physician after another, but all to no purpose. He then visited towns which were famous for their curative waters, and after having bathed in them all, his disease was more painful than ever.

One night he dreamed that a Presence came to him and said, "Brother, hast thou tried all the means of cure?" and he replied, "I have tried all."

"Nay," said the Presence, "come with me, and I will show thee a healing bath which has escaped thy notice."

The afflicted man followed, and the Presence led him to a clear pool of water, and said, "Plunge thyself into this water and thou shalt surely recover," and thereupon vanished.

The man plunged into the water, and on coming out, lo! his disease had left him, and at the same moment he saw written above the pool the word "Renounce." Upon waking the full meaning of his dream flashed across his mind, and looking within he discovered that he had, all along, been a victim to an enervating indulgence, and he vowed that he would renounce it forever. He carried out his vow and from that day his affliction began to leave him, and in a short time he was restored to health.

### *The Link Between Health and Success*

Many people complain that they have broken down through overwork. In the majority of such cases the breakdown is more frequently the result of foolishly wasted energy. If you would secure health you must learn to work without friction. To become anxious or excited, or to worry over needless details is to invite a breakdown.

Work, whether of brain or body, is beneficial and health-giving, and the person who can work with a steady and calm persistency, freed from all anxiety and worry, and with their mind utterly oblivious to all but the work they have in hand, will not only accomplish far more than the person who is always hurried and anxious, but they will retain their health, a boon which the other quickly forfeits.

True health and true success go together, for they are inseparably intertwined in the thought-realm. As mental harmony produces bodily health, so it also leads to a harmonious sequence in the actual working out of one's plans.

Order your thoughts and you will order your life. Pour the oil of tranquility upon the turbulent waters of the passions and prejudices, and the tempests of misfortune, howsoever they may threaten, will be powerless to wreck the ship of your soul, as it threads its way across the ocean of life. And if that ship be piloted by a cheerful and never-failing faith, its course will be doubly sure, and many perils will pass it by which would otherwise attack it.

## The Power of Faith

By the power of faith every enduring work is accomplished. Faith in the Supreme; faith in the overruling Law; faith in your work, and in your power to accomplish that work—here is the rock upon which you must build if you would achieve, if you would stand and not fall.

To follow, under all circumstances, the highest promptings within you; to be always true to the divine self; to rely upon the inward Light, the inward Voice, and to pursue your purpose with a fearless and restful heart, believing that the future will yield unto you the reward of every thought and effort; knowing that the laws of the universe can never fail, and that your own will come back to you with mathematical exactitude, this is faith and the living of faith.

By the power of such faith the dark waters of uncertainty are divided, every mountain of difficulty crumbles away, and the believing soul passes on unharmed.

Strive, O reader, to acquire, above everything, the priceless possession of this dauntless faith, for it is the talisman of happiness, of success, of peace, of power, of all that makes life great and superior to suffering. Build upon such a faith, and you build upon the Rock of the Eternal, and with the materials of the Eternal, and the structure that you erect will never be dissolved, for it will transcend all the accumulations of material luxuries and riches, the end of which is dust.

Whether you are hurled into the depths of sorrow, or lifted upon the heights of joy, ever retain your hold upon this faith, ever return to it as your rock of refuge, and keep your feet firmly planted upon its immortal and immovable base. Centered in such a faith, you will shatter, like so many toys of glass, all the forces of evil that are hurled against you, and you will achieve a success such as the mere striver after worldly gain can never know or even dream of.

"If ye have faith, and doubt not, ye shall not only do this....but if ye shall say unto this mountain, be thou removed and be thou cast into the sea, it shall be done."

### Faith Brings Success

There are those today, men and women tabernacled in flesh and blood, who have realized this faith, who live in it and by it day by day, and who, having put it to the uttermost test, have entered into the possession of its glory and peace. Such have sent out the word of command, and the mountains of sorrow and disappointment, of mental weariness and physical pain have passed from them, and they have been cast into the sea of oblivion.

If you will become possessed of this faith, you will not need to trouble about your future success or failure, and success will come. You will not need to become anxious about results, but will work joyfully and peacefully, knowing that right thoughts and right efforts will inevitably bring about right results.

I know a lady who has entered into many blissful satisfactions, and recently a friend remarked to her,

"Oh, how fortunate you are! You only have to wish for a thing, and it comes to you."

And it did, indeed, appear so on the surface; but in reality all the blessedness that has entered into this woman's life is the direct outcome of the inward state of blessedness which she has, throughout life, been cultivating and training towards perfection. Mere wishing brings nothing but disappointment; it is living that tells. The foolish wish and grumble; the wise, work and wait.

And this woman had worked, worked without and within, but especially within upon heart and soul; and with the invisible hands of the spirit she had built up, with the precious stones of faith, hope, joy, devotion, and love, a fair temple of light, whose glorifying radiance was ever round about her. It beamed in her eye; it shone through her countenance; it vibrated in her voice; and all who came into her presence felt its captivating spell.

## You Create Your Own Fate

And as with her, so with you. Your success, your failure, your influence, your whole life you carry about with you, for your dominant trends of thought are the determining factors in your destiny. Send forth loving, stainless, and happy thoughts, and blessings will fall into your hands, and your table will be spread with the cloth of peace. Send forth hateful, impure, and unhappy thoughts, and curses will rain down upon you, and fear and unrest will wait upon your pillow.

You are the unconditional maker of your fate, be that fate what it may. Every moment you are sending forth from you influences which will make or mar your life. Let your heart grow large and loving and unselfish, and great and lasting will be your influence and success, even though you make little money. Confine it within the narrow limits of self-interest, and even though you become a millionaire your influence and success, at the final reckoning will be found to be utterly insignificant.

Cultivate, then, this pure and unselfish spirit, and combine with purity and faith, singleness of purpose, and you are evolving from within the elements, not only of abounding health and enduring success, but of greatness and power.

### *The Secret of True Power*

If your present position is distasteful to you, and your heart is not in your work, nevertheless perform your duties with scrupulous diligence, and while resting your mind in the idea that the better position and greater opportunities are waiting for you, ever keep an active mental outlook for budding possibilities, so that when the critical moment arrives, and the new channel presents itself, you will step into it with your mind fully prepared for the undertaking, and with that intelligence and foresight which is born of mental discipline.

Whatever your task may be, concentrate your whole mind upon it, throw into it all the energy of which you are capable. The faultless completion of small tasks leads inevitably to larger tasks. See to it that you rise by steady climbing, and you will never fall. And herein lies the secret of true power.

Learn, by constant practice, how to conserve your resources, and to concentrate them, at any moment, upon a given point. The foolish waste all their mental and spiritual energy in frivolity, foolish chatter, or selfish argument, not to mention wasteful physical excesses.

## The Power of Passivity

If you would acquire overcoming power you must cultivate poise and passivity. You must be able to stand alone. All power is associated with immovability. The mountain, the massive rock, the storm-tried oak, all speak to us of power, because of their combined solitary grandeur and defiant fixity; while the shifting sand, the yielding twig, and the waving reed speak to us of weakness, because they are movable and non-resistant, and are utterly useless when detached from their fellows. He or she is the person of power who, when all their fellows are swayed by some emotion or passion, remains calm and unmoved.

He or she only is fitted to command and control who has succeeded in commanding and controlling themself. The hysterical, the fearful, the thoughtless and frivolous, let such seek company, or they will fall for lack of support; but the calm, the fearless, the thoughtful, and grave, let such seek the solitude of the forest, the desert, and the mountaintop, and to their power more power will be added, and they will more and more successfully stem the psychic currents and whirlpools which engulf humankind.

Passion is not power; it is the abuse of power, the dispersion of power. Passion is like a furious storm which beats fiercely and wildly upon the embattled rock, while power is like the rock itself, which remains silent and unmoved through it all.

That was a manifestation of true power when Martin Luther, wearied with the persuasions of his fearful friends, who were doubtful as to his safety should he go to Worms, replied, "If there were as many devils in Worms as there are tiles on the house-tops I would go."

And when Benjamin Disraeli broke down in his first Parliamentary speech, and brought upon himself the derision of the House, that was an exhibition of germinal power when he exclaimed, "The day will come when you will consider it an honor to listen to me."

When that young man, whom I knew, passing through continual reverses and misfortunes, was mocked by friends and told to desist from further effort, and he replied, "The time is not far distant when you will marvel at my good fortune and success," he showed that he was possessed of that silent and irresistible power which has taken him over innumerable difficulties, and crowned his life with success.

### Eliminate Triviality from Your Life

If you have not this power, you may acquire it by practice, and the beginning of power is likewise the beginning of wisdom. You must commence by overcoming those purposeless trivialities to which you have hitherto been a willing victim. Boisterous and uncontrolled laughter, slander and idle talk, and joking merely to raise a laugh, all these things must be put on one side as so much waste of valuable energy.

St. Paul never showed his wonderful insight into the hidden laws of human progress to greater advantage than when he warned the Ephesians against "Foolish talking and jesting which is not convenient," for, to dwell habitually in such practices is to destroy all spiritual power and life.

As you succeed in rendering yourself impervious to such mental dissipations you will begin to understand what true power is, and you will then commence to grapple with the more powerful desires and appetites which hold your soul in bondage, and bar the way to power, and your further progress will then be made clear.

### Single-Mindedness is Power

Above all, be of single aim; have a legitimate and useful purpose, and devote yourself unreservedly to it. Let nothing draw you aside; remember that "The double-minded man is unstable in all his ways." Be eager to learn, but slow to beg. Have a thorough understanding of your work, and let it be your own; as you proceed, ever following the inward Guide, the infallible Voice, you will pass on from victory to victory, and will rise step by step to higher resting-places, and your ever-broadening outlook will gradually reveal to you the essential beauty and purpose of life.

Self-purified, health will be yours; self-governed, power will be yours, and all that you do will prosper, for, ceasing to be a disjointed unit, self-enslaved, you will be in harmony with the Great Law, working no longer against, but with, the universal Life, the Eternal Good. And what health you gain it will remain with you; what success you achieve will be beyond all human computation, and will never pass away; and what influence and power you wield will continue to increase throughout the ages, for it will be a part of that unchangeable Principle which supports the universe.

This, then, is the secret of health—a pure heart and a well-ordered mind; this is the secret of success—an unfaltering faith, and a wisely directed purpose; and to rein in, with unfaltering will, the dark steed of desire, this is the secret of power.

# The Secret of Abounding Happiness

GREAT IS THE THIRST for happiness, and equally great is the lack of happiness. The majority of the poor long for riches, believing that their possession would bring them supreme and lasting happiness. Many who are rich, having gratified every desire and whim, suffer from boredom and repletion, and are farther from the possession of happiness even than the very poor.

If we reflect upon the state of things, it will ultimately lead us to a knowledge of the all-important truth that happiness is not derived from mere outward possessions, nor misery from the lack of them; for if this were so, we should find the poor always miserable, and the rich always happy, whereas the reverse is frequently the case.

Some of the most wretched people whom I have known were those who were surrounded with riches and luxury, while some of the brightest and happiest people I have met were possessed of only the barest necessities of life. Many men who have accumulated riches have confessed that the selfish gratification which followed the acquisition of riches has robbed life of its sweetness, and that they were never so happy as when they were poor.

### The Delusion of Desire

What, then, is happiness, and how is it to be secured? Is it a figment, a delusion, and is suffering alone perennial?

We shall find, after earnest observation and reflection, that all, except those who have entered the way of wisdom, believe that happiness is only to be obtained *by the gratification of desire*. It is this belief, rooted in the soil of ignorance, and continually watered by selfish cravings, that is the cause of all the misery in the world.

And I do not limit the word *desire* to the grosser animal cravings; it extends to the higher psychic realm where far more powerful, subtle, and insidious cravings hold in bondage the intellectual and refined, depriving them of all that beauty, harmony and purity of soul whose expression is happiness.

Most people will admit that selfishness is the cause of all the unhappiness in the world, but they fall under the soul-destroying delusion that it is someone else's selfishness, and not their own. When you are willing to admit that all your unhappiness is the result of your own selfishness you will not be far from the gates of Paradise; but so long as you are convinced that it is the selfishness of others that is robbing you of joy, so long will you remain a prisoner in your self-created purgatory.

Happiness is that inner state of perfect satisfaction which is joy and peace, and from which all desire is eliminated. The satisfaction which results from gratified desire is brief and illusionary, and is always followed by an increased demand for gratification.

Desire is as insatiable as the ocean, and clamors louder and louder as its demands are attended to. It claims ever-increasing service from its deluded devotees, until at last they are struck down with physical or mental anguish, and are hurled into the purifying fires of suffering.

Desire is the region of hell, and all torments are centered there. The giving-up of desire is the realization of heaven, and all delights await the pilgrim there.

> *I sent my soul through the invisible*
> *Some letter of that afterlife to spell*
> *And by and by my soul returned to me,*
> *And whispered, "I myself am heaven and hell."*

### Heaven and Hell Are States of Mind

Heaven and hell are inward states. Sink into self and all its gratifications, and you sink into hell; rise above that state of consciousness which is the utter denial and forgetfulness of self, and you enter heaven.

Self is blind, without judgement, not possessed of true knowledge, and always leads to suffering. Correct perception, unbiased judgement, and true knowledge belong only to the divine state, and only insofar as you realize this divine consciousness can you know what real happiness is.

So long as you persist in selfishly seeking for your own personal happiness, so long will happiness elude you and you will be sowing the seeds of wretchedness. Insofar as you succeed in losing yourself in the service of others, in that measure will happiness come to you, and you will reap a harvest of bliss.

*It is in loving, not in being loved,*
*The heart is blessed;*
*It is in giving, not in seeking gifts,*
*We find out quest.*
*Whatever be thy longing or thy need,*
*That do thou give;*
*So shall thy soul be fed, and thou indeed*
*Shalt truly live.*

### Giving Up to Gain

Cling to self, and you cling to sorrow; relinquish self, and you enter into peace. To seek selfishly is not only to lose happiness, but even that which we believe to be the source of happiness. See how the glutton is continually looking about for a new delicacy wherewith to stimulate his deadened appetite; and how, bloated, burdened, and diseased, scarcely any food at last is eaten with pleasure.

Whereas, he who has mastered his appetite, and not only does not seek, but never thinks of gustatory pleasure, finds delight in the most frugal meal. The angel-form of happiness, which men, looking through the eyes of self, imagine they see in gratified desire, when embraced is always found to be the skeleton of misery. Truly, "He that seeketh his life shall lose it, and he that loseth his life shall find it."

Abiding happiness will come to you when, ceasing to selfishly cling, you are willing to give up. When you are willing to lose, unreservedly, that impermanent thing which is so dear to you, and which, whether you cling to it or not, will one day be snatched from you, then you will find what seemed to you like a painful loss, turns out to be a supreme gain. To give up in order to gain; to be willing to yield up and to suffer loss, this is indeed the Way of Life.

## The Search for Happiness

How is it possible to find real happiness by centering ourselves in those things which, by their nature, must pass away? Abiding and real happiness can only be found by centering ourselves in that which is permanent.

Rise, therefore, above the clinging to and the craving for impermanent things, and you will then enter into a consciousness of the Eternal, and as, rising above the self, and by growing more and more in the spirit of purity, self-sacrifice and universal Love, you become centered in that consciousness, you will realize that happiness which has no reaction, and which can never be taken from you.

The heart that has reached utter self-forgetfulness in its love for others has not only become possessed of the highest happiness, but has entered into immortality, for it has realized the Divine. Look back upon your life, and you will find that the moments of supremest happiness were those in which you uttered some word, or performed some act of compassion or self-denying love.

Spiritually, happiness and harmony are synonymous. Harmony is one phase of the Great Law whose spiritual expression is love. All selfishness is discord, and to be selfish is to be out of harmony with the Divine order. As we realize that all-embracing love which is a negation of self, we put ourselves in harmony with the divine music, the universal song, and that ineffable melody. True happiness becomes our own.

Men and women are rushing hither and thither in the blind search for happiness, and cannot find it; nor ever will until they recognize that happiness is already within them and round about them, filling the universe, and that they, in their selfish searching, are shutting themselves out of it.

**The Secret of Happiness**

> *I followed happiness to make her mine,*
> *Past towering oak and swinging ivy vine.*
> *She fled, I chased, over slanting hill and dale,*
> *Over fields and meadows, in the purpling vale*
> *Pursuing rapidly over dashing stream,*
> *I scaled the dizzy cliffs where eagles scream;*
> *I traversed swiftly every land and sea,*
> *But always happiness eluded me.*
> *Exhausted, fainting, I pursued no more,*
> *But sank to rest upon the barren shore.*
> *One came and asked for food, and one for alms;*
> *I placed the bread and gold in bony palms;*
> *One came for sympathy, and one for rest;*
> *I shared with every needy one my best;*
> *When, lo! sweet Happiness, with form divine,*
> *Stood by me, whispering softly, "I am thine."*

These beautiful lines of Burleigh's express the secret of all-abounding happiness. Sacrifice the personal and transient, and you will rise at once into the impersonal and permanent. Give up that narrow cramped self that seeks to render all things subservient to its own petty interests, and you will enter into the company of the angels, into the very heart and essence of universal Love.

Forget yourself entirely in the sorrows of others and in ministering to others, and divine happiness will emancipate you from all sorrow and suffering. "Taking the first step with a good thought, the second with a good word, and the third with a good deed, I entered Paradise." And you also may enter into Paradise by pursuing the same course. It is not beyond, it is here. It is realized only by the unselfish. It is known in its fullness only to the pure in heart.

If you have not realized this unbounded happiness you may begin to actualize it by ever holding before you the lofty ideal of unselfish love, and aspiring towards it. Aspiration or prayer is desire turned upward. It is the soul turning towards its Divine source, where alone permanent satisfaction can be found. By aspiration the destructive forces of desire are transmuted into divine and all-pervading energy. To aspire is to make an effort to shake off the trammels of desire; it is the prodigal made wise by loneliness and suffering, returning to his Father's Mansion.

### The Joy of Giving

As you rise above the sordid self; as you break, one after another, the chains that bind you, will you realize the joy of giving, as distinguished from the misery of grasping—giving of your substance; giving your intellect; giving the love and light that are growing within you. You will then understand that it is indeed "more blessed to give than to receive." But the giving must be *of the heart* without any taint of self, without desire for reward.

The gift of pure love is always attended with bliss. If, after you have given, you are wounded because you are not thanked or flattered, or your name put in the paper, know that the gift was prompted by vanity and not by love, and you were merely giving in order to get; were not really giving, but grasping.

Lose yourself in the welfare of others; forget yourself in all that you do; this is the secret of abounding happiness.

Ever be on the watch against selfishness, and learn faithfully the divine lessons of inward sacrifice; so shall you climb the highest heights of happiness, and shall remain in the never-clouded sunshine of universal joy, clothed in the shining garment of immortality.

# The Realization
of Prosperity

I T IS GRANTED ONLY TO THE HEART that abounds
with integrity, trust, generosity and love to realize true prosperity. The heart that is not possessed of these qualities cannot know prosperity, for
prosperity, like happiness, is not an outward possession, but an inward realization.

The greedy man may become a millionaire, but he
will always be wretched, and mean and poor, and will
even consider himself outwardly poor so long as there
is a man in the world who is richer than himself, while
the upright, the open-handed and loving will realize a
full and rich prosperity, even though their outward
possessions may be small. *He is poor who is dissatisfied;
he is rich who is contented with what he has, and he is
richer who is generous with what he has.*

When we contemplate the fact that the universe is abounding in all good things, material as well as spiritual, and compare it with man's blind eagerness to secure a few gold coins, or a few acres of dirt, it is then that we realize how dark and ignorant selfishness is; it is then that we know that self-seeking is self-destruction.

Nature gives all, without reservation, and loses nothing; man or woman, grasping all, loses everything.

## True Prosperity

If you would realize true prosperity do not settle down, as many have done, into the belief that if you do right everything will go wrong. Do not allow the word "competition" to shake your faith in the supremacy of righteousness. I care not what people say about the "laws of competition," for do I not know the Unchangeable Law, which shall one day put them all to rout even now in the heart and life of the righteous person? And knowing this Law I can contemplate all dishonesty with undisturbed repose, for I know where certain destruction awaits it.

Under all circumstances *do that which you believe to be right*, and trust the Law; trust the Divine Power that is immanent in the universe, and it will never desert you, and you will always be protected. By such a trust all your losses will be converted into gains, and all curses which threaten will be transmuted into blessings. Never let go of integrity, generosity, and love, for these, coupled with energy, will lift you into the truly prosperous state.

Do not believe the world when it tells you that you must always attend to "number one" first, and to others afterwards. To do this is not to think of others at all, but only of one's own comforts. To those who practice this the day will come when they will be deserted by all, and when they cry out in their loneliness and anguish there will be no one to hear and help them. To consider oneself before all others is to cramp and warp and hinder every noble and divine impulse. Let your soul expand, let your heart reach out to others in loving and generous warmth, and great and lasting will be your joy, and all prosperity will come to you.

Those who have wandered from the highway of righteousness guard themselves against competition; those who always pursue the right need not to trouble about such a defense. This is no empty statement. There are men today who, by the power of integrity and faith, have defied all competition, and who, without swerving in the least from their methods, when competed with, have risen steadily into prosperity, while those who tried to undermine them have fallen back defeated.

To possess those inward qualities which constitute *goodness* is to be armored against all the powers of evil, and to be doubly protected in every time of trial; and to build oneself up in those qualities is to build up a success which cannot be shaken, and to enter into a prosperity which will endure forever.

BOOK
THREE

The Mastery
of Destiny

# TABLE OF CONTENTS

# Preface

THE DISCOVERY OF THE LAW OF EVOLUTION in the material world has prepared men for a knowledge of the law of cause and effect in the mental world. Thought is not less orderly and progressive than the material forms which embody thought; and not alone cells and atoms, but thoughts and deeds are charged with a cumulative and selective energy.

In the realm of thought and deed, the good survives, for it is "fittest"; the evil ultimately perishes. To know that the "perfect law" of Causation is as all-embracing in mind as in matter, is to be relieved from all anxiety concerning the ultimate destiny of individuals and of humanity—

*For man is man and master of his fate—*

and the will in man and woman which is conquering the knowledge of natural law will conquer the knowledge of spiritual law, the will which, in ignorance, chooses evil, will as wisdom evolves and emerges, choose good.

In the universe of law, the final mastery of evil by humankind is assured. The lesser destinies of separation and sorrow, defeat and death, are but disciplinary steps leading to the great Destiny of triumphal mastery. Each of us is unconsciously building, albeit with lacerated hands and labor-bowed form, the Temple of Glory which is to afford us an eternal habitation of peace.

> *Thou art no longer grim, O Destiny!*
> *No longer art thou drear and dark and dread,*
> *Absolute king and god arbitrary*
> *Seated in tragic state among the dead—*
> *Friendly and fair to humankind I see thee now,*
> > *And light and beauty round thy*
> > *lordly brow.*

# Deeds, Character
# & Destiny

THERE IS, AND ALWAYS HAS BEEN, a widespread belief in Fate, or Destiny, that is, in an external and inscrutable power which apportions definite ends to both individuals and nations. This belief has arisen from long observation of the facts of life. Men are conscious that there are certain occurrences which they cannot control and are powerless to avert.

Birth and death, for instance, are inevitable, and many of the incidents of life appear equally inevitable. Men strain every nerve for the attainment of certain ends, and gradually they become conscious of a Power which seems to be not of themselves, which frustrates their puny efforts, and laughs, as it were, at their fruitless striving and struggle.

As men advance in life, they learn to submit, more

or less, to this overruling Power which they do not understand, perceiving only its effects in themselves and the world around them, and they call it by various names, such as God, Providence, Fate, Destiny, etc.

Those of contemplation, such as poets and philosophers, step aside, as it were, to watch the movements of this mysterious Power as it seems to elevate its favorites on the one hand, and strike down its victims on the other, without reference to merit or demerit.

The greatest poets, especially the dramatic poets, represent this power in their works, as they observed it in Nature. The Greek and Roman dramatists usually depict their heros as having foreknowledge of their fate, and taking means to escape it; but by so doing they blindly involve themselves in a series of consequences which bring about the doom which they are trying to avert.

Shakespeare's characters, on the other hand, are represented, as in Nature, with no foreknowledge (except in the form of premonition) of their particular destiny. Thus, according to the poets, whether the person knows their fate or not, they cannot avert it, and every conscious or unconscious act of theirs is a step towards it.

Omar Khayyam's "Moving Finger" is a vivid expression of this idea of Fate:

*The moving Finger writes, and having writ,*
*Moves on: nor all thy Piety nor Wit*
*Shall lure it back to cancel half a line,*
*Nor all thy Tears wash out a Word of it.*

Thus, men and women in all nations and times have experienced in their lives the action of this invisible Power or Law, and in our nation today this experience has been crystallized in the terse proverb, "Man proposes, God disposes."

### Destiny Versus Free Will

But, contradictory as it may appear, there is an equally widespread belief in our responsibility as a free agent.

All moral teaching is an affirmation of our freedom to choose our course and mold our destiny; and humankind's patient and untiring efforts in achieving its ends are declarations of consciousness of freedom and power. This dual experience of fate on the one hand, and freedom on the other, has given rise to the interminable controversy between the believers of Fatalism and the upholders of Free Will—a controversy which was recently revived under the term "Determinism *versus* Free Will."

Between apparently conflicting extremes there is always a "middle way" of balance, justice or compensation which, while it includes both extremes, cannot be said to be either one or the other, and which brings both into harmony; and this middle way is the point of contact between two extremes.

Truth cannot be partisan, but, by its nature, is the Reconciler of extremes; and so, in the matter which we are considering, there is a "golden mean" which brings Fate and Free Will into a close relationship, wherein, indeed, it is seen that these two indisputable facts in human life, for such they are, are but two aspects of one central law, one unifying and all-embracing principle, namely, *the law of causation in its moral aspect.*

## Cause is Free Will; Destiny is Effect

Moral causation necessitates both Fate and Free Will, both individual responsibility and individual predestiny, for the law of causes must also be the law of effects, and the cause and effect must always be equal; the train of causation, both in matter and mind, must be eternally balanced, therefore eternally just, eternally perfect. Thus every effect may be said to be a thing *preordained*, but the predetermining power is a cause, and not the fiat of an arbitrary will.

We each find ourselves involved in the train of causation. Our lives are made up of causes and effects. It is both a sowing and a reaping. Each act of ours is a cause which must be balanced by its effects. We choose the cause (this is Free Will), we cannot choose, alter, or avert the effect (this is Fate); thus Free Will stands for the power to initiate causes, and destiny is involvement in effects.

It is therefore true that each man and woman is predestined to certain ends, but they themselves have (though they know it not) issued the mandate; that good or evil thing from which there is no escape, we have, by our own deeds, brought about.

## *Character is Destiny Itself*

It may here be argued that man and woman are not responsible for their deeds, that these are the effects of their character, and that they are not responsible for the character, good or bad, which was given them at their birth. If character was "given them" at birth, this would be true, and there would then be no moral law, and no need for moral teaching; but characters are not given ready-made, they are *evolved*; they are, indeed, effects, the products of the moral law itself, that is—the products of deeds.

Character is the combined result of an incalculable number of deeds, is, in reality, an accumulation of deeds which has been piled up, so to speak, by the individual during vast ages of time and through innumerable lives, by a slow process of orderly evolution. A man's or woman's birth into this life, with their complex character, to which they consider themself irresponsibly predestined, was determined by their own deeds in former lives.

Each of us is the doer of our own deeds; as such we are the maker of our own character; and as the doer of our deeds and the maker of our character, we are the molder and shaper of our destiny. We have the power to modify and alter our deeds, and every time we act we modify our character, and with the modification of our character for good or evil, we are predetermining for ourself new destinies—destinies disastrous or beneficent in accordance with the nature of our deeds.

Character is destiny itself; as a fixed combination of deeds, it bears within itself the results of those deeds. These results lie hidden as moral seeds in the dark recesses of the character, awaiting their season of germination, growth, and fruitage.

## Destiny is Perfect Justice

Those things which befall a person are reflections of themself; that destiny which pursued them, which they were powerless to escape by effort, or avert by prayer, was the relentless ghoul of their own wrong deeds demanding and enforcing restitution; those blessings and curses which come to them unbidden are the reverberating echoes of the sounds which they themself sent forth.

It is this knowledge of the Perfect Law working through and above all things; of the Perfect Justice operating in and adjusting all human affairs, that enables the good man to love his enemies, and to rise above all hatred, resentment and complaining; for he knows that only his own can come to him, and that, though he be surrounded by persecutors, his enemies are but the blind instruments of a faultless retribution; and so he blames them not, but calmly receives his accounts, and patiently pays his moral debts.

But this is not all; he does not merely pay his debts; he takes care not to contract any further debts. He watches himself and makes his deeds faultless. While paying off evil accounts, he is laying up good accounts. By putting an end to his own errors, he is bringing evil and suffering to an end.

## *The Workings of Destiny*

And now let us consider how the Law operates in particular instances in the outworking of destiny through deeds and character. First, we will look at this present life, for the present is the synthesis of the entire past; the net result of all that a person has ever thought and done is contained within them.

It is noticeable that sometimes the good person fails and the unscrupulous person prospers—a fact which seems to put all moral maxims as to the good results of righteousness out of account—and because of this, many people deny the operation of any just law in human life, and even declare that it is chiefly the unjust that prosper. Nevertheless, the moral law exists, and is not altered or subverted by shallow conclusions.

It should be remembered that each man and woman is *a changing, evolving being*. The good person was not always good; the bad person was not always bad. Even in this life (without, for the moment, going back to former lives), there was a time, in a large number of instances, when the person who is now just, was unjust; when the one who is now kind, was cruel; when the one who is now pure, was impure.

Obversely, there was a time in this life, in a number of instances, when the one who is now unjust, was just; when the one who is now cruel, was kind; when the one who is now impure, was pure.

Thus, the good person who is overtaken with calamity today is reaping the result of their former evil sowing; later they will reap the happy result of their present good sowing; while the bad person is now reaping the result of their former good sowing; later they will reap the result of his present sowing of bad.

But when just causes (of the effects which we see) are not apparent in this life, then they were set going in former lives; and, indeed, the entire evolution of any being, through innumerable births and deaths and ever-enlarging destinies, may be regarded as one long, extended, unbroken line of causes and effects; one indestructible, ever-growing, ever-changing, and ascending life.

### *Character is a Combination of Habits*

Characteristics are fixed habits of the mind, the results of deeds. An act repeated a large number of times becomes unconscious, or automatic—that is, it then seems to repeat itself without any effort on the part of the doer, so that it seems to him almost impossible not to do it, and then it has become a mental characteristic.

Thus, the character of an individual at birth is a combination of habits which he himself has built up by his own thoughts and acts during the course of his evolution, and in accordance with his efforts in this life will his character be modified for good or evil in the future.

Here is a poor man out of work. He is honest, and he is not a shirker. He wants work, and cannot get it. He tries hard, and continues to fail. Where is the justice in his lot?

There was a time in this man's condition when he had plenty of work. He felt burdened with it; he shirked it, and longed for ease. He thought how delightful it would be to have nothing to do. He did not appreciate the blessedness of his lot. His desire for ease is now gratified, but the fruit for which he longed, and which he thought would taste so sweet, has turned to ashes in his mouth.

The condition which he aimed for, namely, to have nothing to do, he has reached, and there he is compelled to remain till his lesson is thoroughly learned. And he is surely learning that habitual ease is degrading, that to have nothing to do is a condition of wretchedness, and that work is a noble and blessed thing.

His former desires and deeds have brought him where he is; and now his present desire for work, his ceaseless searching and asking for it, will just as surely bring about its own beneficent result. No longer desiring idleness, his present condition will, as an effect, the cause of which is no longer propagated, soon pass away, and he will obtain employment; and if his whole mind is now set on work, and he desires it above all else, then when it comes he will be overwhelmed with it; it will flow in to him from all sides, and he will prosper in his industry. Then, if he does not understand the law of cause and effect in human life, he will wonder why work comes to him apparently unsought, while others who seek it strenuously fail to obtain it.

### Sweet and Bitter Fruits

Nothing comes unbidden; where the shadow is, there also is the substance. That which comes to the individual is the product of his own deeds. As cheerful industry leads to greater industry and increasing prosperity, and labor shirked or undertaken discontentedly leads to a lesser degree of labor and decreasing prosperity, so all the varied conditions of life as we see them—they are *the effects of deeds*, destinies wrought by the thoughts and deeds of each particular individual.

So also with the vast variety of characters—they are the ripening and ripened growth of the sowing of deeds, a sowing not confined solely to this visible life, but going backward through that infinite life which traverses the portals of innumerable births and deaths, and which also will extend into the illimitable future, reaping its own harvests, eating the sweet and bitter fruits of its own deeds.

It is thus literally true that when men die they "go to heaven or hell," in accordance with their deeds. But the heaven and hell are in this world.

The rich man who abused his wealth or who obtained his riches by fraud or oppression, is reborn in poverty and shame. The poor man who used the little he possessed wisely and unselfishly is reborn in plenty and honor. The cruel and unjust are reborn in the midst of harsh and untoward surroundings; the kind and just are reborn where kind hearts and gentle hands watch over and tend them. Thus, with every vice and virtue, each receives its own; each declares its own destiny.

## A School for the Development of Character

But even those who refuse to believe in rebirth will find that even in this life men almost invariably reap what they sow; and the time is surely coming when social and political reformers will pay more attention to the development of character than the mere gaining of party issues.

As the individual reaps what he sows, so the nation, being a community of individuals, reaps also what it sows. Nations become great when their leaders are just men; they fall and fade when their just men pass away. Those who are in power set an example, good or bad, for the entire nation.

Great will be the peace and prosperity of a nation when there shall arise within it a line of statesmen who, having first established themselves in a lofty integrity of character, shall direct the energies of the nation toward the culture of virtue and development of character, knowing that only through personal industry, integrity, and nobility can national prosperity proceed.

Still, above all, is the Great Law, calmly and with

infallible justice meting out to mortals their fleeting destinies, tear-stained or smiling, the fabric of their hands. Life is a great school for the development of character, and all, through strife and struggle, vice and virtue, success and failure, are slowly but surely learning the lessons of wisdom.

# The Science of
# Self-Control

WE LIVE IN A SCIENTIFIC AGE. Men of science are numbered by thousands, and they are ceaselessly searching, analyzing, and experimenting with a view to discovery and the increase of knowledge. The shelves of our libraries, both public and private, are heavy with their load of imposing volumes on scientific subjects, and the wonderful achievements of modern science are always before us—whether in our homes or in our streets, in country or town, on land or sea—there shall we have before us some marvelous device, some recent accomplishment of science, for adding to our comfort, increasing our speed, or saving the labor of our hands.

Yet, with all our vast store of scientific knowledge, and its startling and rapidly increasing results in the world of discovery and invention, there is, in this age, one branch of science which has so far fallen into decay as to have become almost forgotten; a science, nevertheless, which is of greater importance than all the other sciences combined, and without which all science would but subserve the ends of selfishness, and aid in humankind's destruction—I refer to the science of Self-control.

## Acquiring Spiritual Power

Our modern scientists study the elements and forces which are outside themselves, with the object of controlling and utilizing them. The ancients studied the elements and forces which were within themselves, with a view to controlling and utilizing them, and the ancients produced such mighty Masters of knowledge in this direction, that to this day they are held in reverence as gods, and the vast religious organizations of the world are based upon their achievements.

Wonderful as are the forces in nature, they are vastly inferior to that combination of intelligent forces which comprise the human mind, and which dominate and direct the blind mechanical forces of nature. Therefore, it follows that, to understand, control, and direct the inner forces of passion, desire, will and intellect, is to be in possession of the destinies of men and nations.

As in ordinary science, there are, in this divine science, degrees of attainment; and a man is great in knowledge, great in himself, and great in his influence on the world, in the measure that he is great in self-control.

He who understands and dominates the forces of external nature is the natural scientist; but he who understands and dominates the internal forces of the mind is the divine scientist; and the laws which operate in gaining a knowledge of external appearances, operate also in gaining a knowledge of internal verities.

A man cannot become an accomplished scientist in a few weeks or months, nay not even a few years. But only after many years of painstaking investigation can he speak with authority, and be ranked among the masters of science. Likewise, a man cannot acquire self-control, and become possessed of the wisdom and peace-giving knowledge which that self-control confers, but by many years of patient labor; a labor which is all the more arduous because it is silent, and both unrecognized and unappreciated by others; and he who would pursue this science successfully must learn to stand alone, and to toil unrewarded, as far as any outward profit is concerned.

## *The Five Scientific Steps*

The natural scientist pursues, in acquiring his particular kind of knowledge, the following five orderly and sequential steps:

1. *Observation*: that is, he closely and persistently observes the facts of nature.

2. *Experiment*: Having become acquainted, by repeated observations, with certain facts, he experiments with those facts, with a view to the discovery of natural laws. He puts his facts through rigid processes of analysis, and so finds out what is useless and what of value; and he rejects the former and retains the latter.

3. *Classification*: Having accumulated and verified a mass of facts by numberless observations and experiments, he commences to classify those facts, to arrange them in orderly groups with the object of discovering some underlying law, some hidden and unifying principle, which governs, regulates, and binds together these facts.

4. **Deduction:** Thus he passes on to the fourth step of deduction. From the facts and results which are before him, he discovers certain invariable modes of action, and thus reveals the hidden laws of things.

5. **Knowledge:** Having proven and established certain laws, it may be said of such a man that he *knows*. He is a scientist, a man of knowledge.

But the attainment of scientific knowledge is not the end, great as it is. Men do not attain knowledge for themselves alone, nor to keep it locked secretly in their hearts, like a beautiful jewel in a dark chest. The end of such knowledge is use, service, the increase of the comfort and happiness of the world. Thus, when a man has become a scientist, he gives the world the benefit of his knowledge, and unselfishly bestows upon mankind the results of his labors. Thus, beyond knowledge, there is a further step of *Use*: that is, the right and unselfish use of the knowledge acquired; the application of knowledge to invention for the common good.

### The Divine Scientist

It will be noted that the five steps or processes enumerated follow in a orderly succession, and that no man can become a scientist who omits any one of them. Without the first step of systematic observation, for instance, he could not even enter the realm of knowledge of nature's secrets.

At first, the searcher for such knowledge has before him a universe of *things*: these things he does not understand; many of them, indeed, seem to be irreconcilably opposed one to the other, and there is apparent confusion; but by patiently and laboriously pursuing these five processes, he discovers the order, nature, and essences of things; perceives the central law or laws which bind them together in harmonious relationship, and so puts an end to confusion and ignorance.

As with the natural scientist, so with the divine scientist; he must pursue, with the same self-sacrificing diligence, five progressive steps in the attainment of self-knowledge, self-control. These five steps are the same as with the natural scientist, but *the process is reversed*, the mind, instead of being centered upon external things, is turned back upon itself, and the investigations are pursued in the realm of mind (of one's own mind) instead of in that of matter.

At first, the searcher for divine knowledge is confronted with that mass of desires, passions, emotions, ideas, and intellections which he calls himself, which is the basis of all his actions, and from which his life proceeds. This combination of invisible, yet powerful, forces appears confusedly; some of them stand, apparently, in direct conflict with each other, without any appearance or hope of reconciliation; his mind in its entirety, too, with his life which proceeds from that mind, does not seem to have any equitable relation to many other minds and lives about him, and altogether there is a condition of pain and confusion from which he would gladly escape.

## The Five Divine Scientist Steps

Thus, the divine scientist begins by keenly realizing his state of ignorance, for no one could acquire either natural or divine knowledge, if he were convinced that without study or labor he already possessed it. With such perception of one's ignorance there comes a desire for knowledge, and the novice in self-control enters upon the ascending pathway, in which are the following five steps:

1. *Introspection.* This coincides with the observation of the natural scientist. The mental eye is turned like a searchlight upon the inner things of

the mind, and its subtle and ever-varying process-es are observed and carefully noted. This step-ping aside from selfish gratifications, from the excitements of worldly pleasures and ambitions, in order to observe, with the object of under-standing one's nature, is the beginning of self-control. Hitherto, the man has been blindly and impotently borne along by the impulses of his nature, the mere creature of things and circum-stances, but now he puts a check upon his impulses and, instead of being controlled, begins to control.

2. *Self-analysis.* Having observed the tendencies of the mind, they are then closely examined, and are put through a rigid process of analysis. The evil ten-dencies (those that produce painful effects) are sep-arated from the good tendencies (those that produce peaceful effects); and the various tenden-cies with the particular actions they produce, and the definite results which invariably spring from these actions, are gradually grasped by the under-standing, which is at last enabled to follow them in their swift and subtle interplay and profound ramifi-cations. It is a process of *testing and proving*, and, for the searcher, a period of being tested and proved.

3. *Adjustment.* By this time, the practical student of things divine has clearly before him every tendency and aspect of his nature, down to the profoundest promptings of his mind, and the most subtle motives of his heart. There is not a spot or corner left, which he has not explored and illuminated with the light of self-examination. He is familiar with every weak and selfish point, every strong and virtuous quality.

It is considered the height of wisdom to be able to see ourselves as others see us, but the practicer of self-control goes far beyond this: he not only sees himself as others see him, he *sees himself as he is.*

Thus, standing face to face with himself, not striving to hide away from any secret fault; no longer defending himself with pleasant flatteries; neither underrating nor overrating himself or his powers, and no more cursed with self-praise or self-pity, he sees the full magnitude of the task which lies before him; sees clearly ahead the heights of self-control, and knows what work he has to do to reach them.

He is no longer in a state of confusion, but has gained a glimpse of the laws which operate in the world of thought, and he now begins to *adjust* his mind in accordance with those laws. This is a process of *weeding, sifting, cleansing.* As the farmer weeds, cleans, and prepares the ground for his crops, so the student removes the weeds of evil from his mind, cleanses and purifies it preparatory to sowing the seeds of righteous actions which shall produce the harvest of a well-ordered life.

4. *Righteousness.* Having adjusted his thoughts and deeds to those minor laws which operate in mental activities in the production of pain and pleasure, unrest and peace, sorrow and bliss, he now perceives that there is involved in those laws one Great Central Law which, like the law of gravitation in the natural world, is supreme in the world of mind; a law to which all thoughts and deeds are subservient, and by which they are regulated and kept in their proper sphere. This is the law of Justice or Righteousness, which is universal and supreme. To this law he now conforms.

Instead of thinking and acting blindly, as the nature is stimulated and appealed to by outward things, he subordinates his thoughts and deeds to this central principle. He no longer acts from self, *but does what is right*—what is universally and eternally right. He is no longer the abject slave of his nature and circumstances, he is the master of his nature and circumstances. He is no longer carried hither and thither on the forces of his mind; he controls and guides these forces to the accomplishment of his purposes. Thus, having his nature in control and subjection, not thinking thoughts or doing deeds which oppose the righteous law, and which, therefore, that law annuls with suffering and defeat above the dominion of sin and sorrow, ignorance and doubt, and is strong, calm and peaceful.

5. *Pure Knowledge.* By thinking right and acting right, he proves, by experience, the existence of the divine law on which the mind is framed, and which is the guiding and unifying principle in all human affairs and events, whether individual or national. Thus, by perfecting himself in self-control, he acquires divine knowledge; he reaches the point where it may be said of him, as of the natural scientist, that he *knows.*

He has mastered the science of self-control, and has brought knowledge out of ignorance, order out of confusion. He has acquired that knowledge of self which includes knowledge of all men; that knowledge of one's own life which embraces knowledge of all lives—for all minds are the same in essence (differing only in degree), are framed upon the same law; and the same thoughts and acts, by whatsoever individual they are wrought, will always produce the same results.

But this divine and peace-bestowing knowledge, as in the case of the natural scientist, is not gained for one's self alone; for if this were so, the aim of evolution would be frustrated, and it is not in the nature of things to fall short of ripening and accomplishment; and, indeed, he who thought to gain this knowledge solely for his own happiness would most surely fail.

So beyond the fifth step of Pure Knowledge, there is a still further one of *Wisdom*, which is the right application of the knowledge acquired; the pouring out upon the world, unselfishly and without stint, the result of one's labors, thus accelerating progress and uplifting humanity.

It may be said of men who have not gone back into their own nature to control and purify it, that they cannot clearly distinguish between good and evil, right and wrong. They reach after those things which they think will give them pleasure, and try to avoid those things which they believe will cause them pain.

The source of their actions is self, and they only discover right painfully and in a fragmentary way, by periodically passing through severe sufferings, and lashings of conscience. But he who practices self-control, passing through the five processes, which are five stages of growth, gains that knowledge which enables him to act from the moral law which sustains the universe. He knows good and evil, right and wrong, and, thus knowing them, lives in accordance with good and right. He no longer needs to consider what is pleasant or what is unpleasant, but does what is right; his nature is in harmony with his conscience, and there is no remorse; his mind is in unison with the Great Law, and there is no more suffering and sin; for him evil is ended, and good is all in all.

# Cause & Effect
# in Human Conduct

IT IS AN AXIOM with the scientists that every
effect is related to a cause. Apply this to the
realm of human conduct, and there is revealed
the principle of justice.

Every scientist knows (and now all men believe)
that perfect harmony prevails throughout every portion of the physical universe, from the speck of dust
to the greatest sun. Everywhere there is exquisite
adjustment. In the sidereal universe, with its millions
of suns rolling majestically through space and carry-
ing with them their respective systems of revolving
planets, its vast nebulae, its seas of meteors, and its
vast army of comets traveling through illimitable
space with inconceivable velocity, perfect order prevails; and again, in the natural world, with its multi-
tudinous aspects of life, and its infinite variety of

forms, there are clearly defined limits of specific laws, through the operation of which all confusion is avoided, and unity and harmony eternally obtain.

If this universal harmony could be arbitrarily broken, even in one small particular, the universe would cease to be; there could be no cosmos, but only universal chaos. Nor can it be possible in such a universe of law that there should exist any personal power which is above, outside, and superior to, such law in the sense that it can defy it, or set it aside; for whatever beings exist, whether they be men or gods, they exist by virtue of such law; and the highest, best, and wisest among beings would manifest his greater wisdom by his more complete obedience to that law which is wiser than wisdom, and than which nothing more perfect could be devised.

All things, whether visible or invisible, are subservient to, and fall within the scope of, this infinite and eternal law of *causation*. As all things seen obey it, so all things unseen—the thoughts and deeds of men, whether secret or open—cannot escape it.

*Do right, it recompenseth; do one wrong,*
*The equal retribution must be made.*

Perfect justice upholds the universe; perfect justice regulates human life and conduct. All the varying conditions of life, as they occur in the world today, are the result of this law reacting on human conduct. Man can (and does) choose what causes he shall set in operation, but he cannot change the nature of effects; he can decide what thoughts he shall think, and what deeds he shall do, but he has no power over the *results* of those thoughts and deeds; these are regulated by the overruling law.

Man has all power to act, but his power ends with the act committed. The result of the act cannot be altered, annulled, or escaped; it is irrevocable. Evil thoughts and deeds produce conditions of suffering; good thoughts and deeds determine conditions of blessedness. Thus man's power is limited to, and his blessedness or misery is determined by, *his own conduct*. To know this truth, renders life simple, plain, and unmistakable; all the crooked paths are straightened out, the heights of wisdom are revealed, and the open door to salvation from evil and suffering is perceived and entered.

### Right and Wrong Solutions to Life

Life may be likened to a sum in arithmetic. It is bewilderingly difficult and complex to the pupil who has not yet grasped the key to its correct solution, but once this is perceived and laid hold of, it becomes as astonishingly simple as it was formerly profoundly perplexing.

Some idea of this relative simplicity and complexity of life may be grasped by fully recognizing and realizing the fact that, while there are scores, and perhaps hundreds, of ways in which a sum may be done wrong, *there is only one way by which it can be done right*, and that when the right way is found the pupil *knows it to be the right*; his perplexity vanishes, and he knows that he has mastered the problem.

It is true that the pupil, while doing his sum incorrectly, may (and frequently does) *think* he has done it correctly, but he is not sure; his perplexity is still there, and if he is an earnest and apt pupil, he will recognize his own error when it is pointed out by the teacher. So in life, men think they are living rightly while they are continuing through ignorance, to live wrongly; but the presence of doubt, perplexity, and unhappiness are sure indications that the right way has not yet been found.

There are foolish and careless pupils who would like to pass a sum as correct before they have acquired a true knowledge of figures, but the eye and skill of the teacher quickly detect and expose the fallacy. So in life there can be no falsifying of results; the eye of the Great Law reveals and exposes. Twice five will make ten to all eternity, and no amount of ignorance, stupidity, or delusion can bring the result up to eleven.

## We Weave Our Garment of Life

If one looks superficially at a piece of cloth, he sees it as a piece of cloth, but if he goes further and inquires into its manufacture, and examines it closely and attentively, he sees that it is composed of a combination of individual threads, and that, while all the threads are interdependent, each thread pursues its own way throughout, never becoming confused with a sister thread. It is this entire absence of confusion between the particular threads which constitutes the finished work *a piece of cloth*; any inharmonious commingling of the thread would result in a bundle of *waste* or a useless *rag*.

Life is like a piece of cloth, and the threads of which it is composed are individual lives. The threads, while being interdependent are not confounded one with the other. Each follows its own course. Each individual suffers and enjoys the consequences of his own deeds, and not the deeds of another. The course of each is simple and definite; the whole forming a complicated, yet harmonious combination of sequences. There are action and reaction, deed and consequence, cause and effect, and the counterbalancing reaction, consequence, and effect is always in exact ratio with the initiatory impulse.

A durable and satisfactory piece of cloth cannot be made from shoddy material, and the threads of selfish thoughts and bad deeds will not produce a useful and beautiful life—a life that will wear well, and bear close inspection.

Each man makes or mars his own life; it is not made or marred by his neighbor, or by anything external to himself. Each thought he thinks, each deed he does, is another thread—shoddy or genuine—woven into the garment of life; and as he makes the garment so must he wear it. He is not responsible for his neighbor's actions; he is responsible only for his own deeds; he is the custodian of his own actions.

### Cause and Effect Are Simultaneous

The "problem of evil" subsists in a man's own evil

deeds, and it is solved when those deeds are purified. Says Rousseau: "Man, seek no longer the origin of evil; thou thyself art its origin."

Effect can never be divorced from cause; it can never be a different nature from cause. Emerson says: "Justice is not postponed; a perfect equity adjusts the balance in all parts of life."

And there is a profound sense in which cause and effect are simultaneous, and form one perfect whole. Thus, upon the instant that a man thinks, say, a cruel thought, or does a cruel deed, that same instant he has *injured his own mind*; he is not the same man he was the previous instant; he is a little viler and a little more unhappy; and a number of such successive thoughts and deeds would produce a cruel and wretched man.

The same thing applies to the contrary—the thinking of a kind thought, or doing a kind deed—an immediate nobility and happiness attend it; the man is better than he was before, and a number of such deeds would produce a great and blissful soul.

Thus individual human conduct determines, by the faultless law of cause and effect, individual merit or demerit, individual happiness or wretchedness. What a man thinks, that he does;

what he does, happiness or wretchedness is that which he is. If he is perplexed, unhappy, restless, or wretched, let him look to himself, for there and nowhere else is the source of all his trouble.

# Training of the Will

**W**ITHOUT STRENGTH of mind, nothing worthy of accomplishment can be done, and the cultivation of that steadiness and stability of character which is commonly called "will-power" is one of the foremost duties of man, for its possession is essentially necessary both to his temporal and eternal well-being. Fixedness of purpose is at the root of all successful efforts, whether in things worldly or spiritual, and without it man cannot be otherwise than wretched, and dependent upon others for that support which should be found within himself.

The mystery which has been thrown around the subject of cultivation of the will by those who advertise to sell "occult advice" on the matter for so many dollars, should be avoided and dispelled, for nothing could be further removed from secrecy and mystery than the practical methods by which alone strength of will can be developed.

The true path of will-cultivation is only to be found in the common everyday life of the individual, and so obvious and simple is it that the majority looking for something complicated and mysterious, pass it by unnoticed.

A little logical thought will soon convince a man that he cannot be both weak and strong at the same time, that he cannot develop a stronger will while remaining a slave to weak indulgences, and that, therefore, the direct and only way to that greater strength is to assail and conquer his weaknesses. All the means for the cultivation of the will are already at hand in the mind and life of the individual; they reside in the weak side of his character, by attacking and vanquishing which the necessary strength of will will be developed.

### Seven Rules to Train the Will

He who has succeeded in grasping this simple preliminary truth, will perceive that the whole science of will-cultivation is embodied in the following seven rules:

1. Break off bad habits.
2. Form good habits.

3. Give scrupulous attention to the duty of the present moment.
4. Do vigorously, and at once, whatever has to be done.
5. Live by rule.
6. Control the tongue.
7. Control the mind.

Anyone who earnestly mediates upon, and diligently practices, the above rules, will not fail to develop that purity of purpose and power of will which will enable him to successfully cope with every difficulty, and pass triumphantly through every emergency.

It will be seen that the first step is the breaking away from bad habits. This is no easy task. It demands the putting forth of great efforts, or a succession of efforts, and it is by such efforts that the will can alone be invigorated and fortified.

If one refuses to take the first step, he cannot increase in will-power, for by submitting to a bad habit, because of the immediate pleasure which it affords, one forfeits the right to rule over himself, and is so far a weak slave. He who thus avoids self-discipline, and looks for some "occult secrets" for gaining will-power at the expenditure of little or no effort on his part, is deluding himself, and is weakening the will-power which he already possesses.

## Forming Good Habits

The increased strength of will which is gained by success in overcoming bad habits enables one to initiate good habits; for, while the conquering of a bad habit requires strength of purpose, the forming of a new one necessitates the *intelligent direction of purpose*. To do this, a man must be mentally active and energetic, and must keep a constant watch upon himself.

As a man succeeds in perfecting himself in the second rule, it will not be very difficult for him to observe the third, that of giving scrupulous attention to the duty of the present moment. Thoroughness is a step in the development of the will which cannot be passed over. Slipshod work is an indication of weakness. Perfection should be aimed at, even in the smallest task. By not dividing the mind, but giving the whole attention to each separate task as it presents itself, singleness of purpose and intense concentration of mind are gradually gained—two mental powers which give weight and worth of character, and bring repose and joy to their possessor.

## *Don't Delay or Postpone*

The fourth rule—that of doing vigorously, and at once, whatever has to be done—is equally important. Idleness and a strong will cannot go together, and procrastination is a total barrier to the acquisition of purposeful action. Nothing should be "put off" until another time, not even for a few minutes. That which ought to be done now should be done now. This seems a little thing, but it is of far-reaching importance. It leads to strength, success and peace.

## *Live by Rules*

The man who is to manifest a cultivated will must also live by certain fixed rules. He must not blindly gratify his passions and impulses, but must school them to obedience. He should live according to principle, and not according to passion. He should decide what he will eat and drink and wear, and what he will not eat and drink and wear; how many meals per day he will have, and at what times he will have them; at what time he will go to bed, and at what time get up.

He should make rules for the right government of his conduct in every department of his life, and should religiously adhere to them. To live loosely and indiscriminately, eating and drinking and sensually indulging at the beck and call of appetite and inclination, is to be a mere animal, and not a man with will and reason.

The beast in man must be scourged and disciplined and brought into subjection, and this can only be done by training the mind and life on certain fixed rules of right conduct. The saint attains to holiness by not violating his vows, and the man who lives according to good and fixed rules, is strong to accomplish his purpose.

### Controlling the Mind

The sixth rule, that of controlling the tongue, must be practiced until one has perfect command of his speech, so that he utters nothing in peevishness, anger, irritability, or with evil intent. The man of strong will does not allow his tongue to run thoughtlessly and without check.

All these six rules, if faithfully practiced, will lead up to the seventh, which is the most important of them all—namely, rightly controlling the mind. Self-control is the most essential thing in life, yet least understood; but he who patiently practices the rules herein laid down, bringing them into requisition in all his ways and undertakings, will learn, by his own experience and efforts, how to control and train the mind, and to earn thereby the supreme crown of manhood—the crown of a perfectly poised will.

## Be Thorough In Little Things

Thoroughness consists in doing little things as though they were the greatest things in the world. That the little things of life are of primary importance, is a truth not generally understood, and the thought that little things can be neglected, thrown aside, or slurred over, is at the root of that lack of thoroughness which is so common, and which results in imperfect work and unhappy lives.

When one understands that the great things of the world and of life consist of a combination of small things, and that without this aggregation of small things the great things would be nonexistent, then he begins to pay careful attention to those things which he formerly regarded as insignificant. He thus acquires the quality of thoroughness, and becomes a man of usefulness and influence; for the possession or nonpossession of this one quality may mean all the difference between a life of peace and power, and one of misery and weakness.

Every employer of labor knows how comparatively rare this quality is—how difficult it is to find men and women who will put thought and energy into their work, and do it completely and satisfactorily. Bad workmanship abounds. Skill and excellence are acquired by few.

Thoughtlessness, carelessness, and laziness are such common vices that it should cease to appear strange that, in spite of "social reform," the ranks of the unemployed should continue to swell, for those who shirk their work today will, another day, in the hour of deep necessity, look and ask for work in vain.

### Excellence is Always in Demand

The law of "the survival of the fittest" is not based on cruelty, it is based on justice; it is one aspect of that divine equity which everywhere prevails. Vice is "beaten with many stripes"; if it were not so, how could virtue be developed? The thoughtless and lazy cannot take precedence of, or stand equally with, the thoughtful and industrious.

A friend of mine tells me that his father gave all his children the following piece of advice: "Whatever your future work may be, put your whole mind upon it and do it thoroughly; you need then have no fear as to your welfare, for there are so many who are careless and negligent that the services of the thorough man are always in demand."

I know those who have, for years, tried almost in vain to secure competent workmanship in spheres which do not require exceptional skill, but which call chiefly for forethought, energy, and conscientious care. They have discharged one after another for negligence, laziness, incompetence, and persistent breaches of duty—not to mention other vices which have no bearing on this subject; yet the vast army of the unemployed continues to cry out against the laws, against society, and against Heaven.

The cause of this common lack of thoroughness is not far to seek; it lies in that thirst for pleasure which not only creates a distaste for steady labor, but renders one incapable of doing the best work and of properly fulfilling one's duty.

A short time ago, a case came under my observation (one of many such), of a poor woman who was given, at her earnest appeal, a responsible and lucrative position. She had been at her post only a few days when she began to talk of the "pleasure trips" she was going to have now she had come to that place. She was discharged at the end of the month for negligence and incompetence.

As two objects cannot occupy the same space at

the same time, so the mind that is occupied with pleasure cannot be concentrated upon the perfect performance of duty. Pleasure has its own place and time, but its consideration should not be allowed to enter the mind during those hours which should be devoted to duty. Those who, while engaged in their worldly task, are continually dwelling upon anticipated pleasures, cannot do otherwise than bungle through their work, or even neglect it when their pleasure seems to be at stake.

### Throw Your Heart into What You Do

Thoroughness is completeness, perfection; it means doing a thing so well that there is nothing left to be desired; it means doing one's work, if not better than anyone else can do it, at least not worse than the best that others do. It means the exercise of much thought, the putting forth of great energy, the persistent application of the mind to its task, the cultivation of patience, perseverance, and a high sense of duty.

An ancient teacher said, "If anything has to be done, let a man do it, let him attack it vigorously"; and another teacher said, "Whatsoever thy hand findeth to do, do it with all thy might."

He who lacks thoroughness in his worldly duties, will also lack the same quality in spiritual things. He will not improve his character; will be weak and half-hearted in his religion, and will not accomplish any good and useful end. The man who keeps one eye on worldly pleasure and the other on religion, and who thinks he can have the advantage of both conditions, will not be thorough either in his pleasure-seeking or his religion, but will make a sorry business of both. It is better to be a whole-souled worldling than a half-hearted religionist; better to give the entire mind to a lower thing than half of it to a higher.

It is preferable to be thorough, even if it be in a bad or selfish direction, rather than inefficient and squeamish in good directions, for thoroughness leads ever rapidly to the development of character and the acquisition of wisdom; it accelerates progress and unfoldment; and while it leads the bad to something better, it spurs the good to higher and ever higher heights of usefulness and power.

# Mind-Building
& Life-Building

EVERYTHING BOTH IN NATURE and the works of man is produced by a process of building. The rock is built up of atoms; the plant, the animal and man are built up of cells; a house is built of bricks, and a book is built of letters. A world is composed of a large number of forms, and a city of a large number of houses. The arts, sciences, and institutions of a nation are built up by the efforts of individuals. The history of a nation is the building of its deeds.

The process of building necessitates the alternate process of breaking down. Old forms that have served their purpose are broken up, and the material of which they are composed enters into new combinations. There is a reciprocal integration and disintegration. In all compounded bodies, old cells are ceaselessly being broken up, and new cells are formed to take their place.

The works of man also require to be continually renewed until they become old and useless, when they are torn down in order that some better purpose may be served. These two processes of breaking down and building up in Nature are called *death and life*; in the artificial works of man they are called *destruction and restoration*.

### Character is Built by Thought

This dual process which occurs universally in things visible, also occurs universally in things invisible. As a body is built of cells, and a house of bricks, so a man's mind is built of thoughts. The various characters of men are none other than compounds of thoughts of varying combinations. Herein we see the deep truth of the saying, "As a man thinketh in his heart, so is he."

Individual characteristics are *fixed processes of thought*; that is, they are fixed in the sense that they have become such an integral part of the character that they can only be altered or removed by a protracted effort of the will, and by much self-discipline.

Character is built in the same way as a tree or a house is built—namely, by the ceaseless addition of new material, and that material is *thought*. By the aid of millions of bricks a city is built; by the aid of millions of thoughts a mind, a character, is built. "Rome was not built in a day," and a Buddha, a Plato, or a Shakespeare is not built in a lifetime.

Every man is a mind-builder, whether he recognizes it or not. Every man must by necessity think, and every thought is another brick laid down in the edifice of mind. Such "brick-laying" is done loosely and carelessly by a vast number of people, the result being unstable and tottering characters that are ready to go down under the first little gust of trouble or temptation.

Some, also, put into the building of their minds large numbers of impure thoughts; there are so many rotten bricks that crumble away as fast as they are put in, leaving always an unfinished and unsightly building, and one which can afford no comfort and no shelter for its possessor.

Debilitating thoughts about one's health, enervating thoughts concerning unlawful pleasures, weakening thoughts of failure, and sickly thoughts of self-pity and self-praise are useless bricks with which no substantial mind-temple can be raised.

### Building a Better Habitation

Pure thoughts, wisely chosen and well placed, are so many durable bricks which will never crumble away, and from which a finished and beautiful building, and one which affords comfort and shelter for its possessor, can be rapidly erected.

Bracing thoughts of strength, of confidence, of duty; inspiring thoughts of a large, free, unfettered, and unselfish life, are useful bricks with which a substantial mind-temple can be raised; and the building of such a temple necessitates that old and useless habits of thought be broken down and destroyed.

*Build thee more stately mansions, O my soul!*
*As the swift seasons roll.*

Each man is the builder of himself. If he is the occupant of a jerry-built hovel of a mind that lets in the rains of many troubles, and through which blow the keen winds of oft-recurring disappointments, let him get to work to build a more noble mansion which will afford him better protection against those mental elements. Trying to weakly shift the responsibility for his jerry-building on the devil, or his forefathers, or anything or anybody but himself, will neither add to his comfort, nor help him to build a better habitation.

When he wakes up to a sense of his responsibility, and an approximate estimate of his power, then he will commence to build like a true workman, and will produce a symmetrical and finished character that will endure, and be cherished by posterity, and which, while affording a never-failing protection for himself, will continue to give shelter to many a struggling one when he has passed away.

## Four Principles

The whole universe is framed on a few mathematical principles. All the wonderful works of man in the material world have been brought about by the rigid observation of a few underlying principles; and all there is to the making of a successful, happy, and beautiful life, is the knowledge and application of a few simple, root principles.

If a man is to erect a building that is to resist the fiercest storms, he must build it on a simple, mathematical principle, or law, such as the square or the circle; if he ignores this, his edifice will topple down even before it is finished.

Likewise, if a man is to build up a successful, strong, and exemplary life—a life that will stoutly resist the fiercest storms of adversity and temptation—it must be framed on a few simple, undeviating moral principles.

Four of these principles are—*Justice, Rectitude, Sincerity*, and *Kindness*. These four ethical truths are to the making of a life what the four lines of a square are to the building of a house. If a man ignores them and thinks to obtain success and happiness and peace by injustice, trickery, and selfishness, he is in the position of a builder who imagines he can build a strong and durable habitation while ignoring the relative arrangement of mathematical lines. He will, in the end, obtain only disappointment and failure.

He may, for a time, make money, which will delude him into believing that injustice and dishonesty pay well; but in reality his life is so weak and unstable that it is ready at any moment to fall; and when a critical period comes, as it must, his affairs, his reputation, and his riches crumble to ruins, and he is buried in his own desolation.

It is totally impossible for a man to achieve a truly successful and happy life who ignores the four moral principles enumerated, whilst the man who scrupulously observes them in all his dealings can no more fail of success and blessedness than the earth can fail of the light and warmth of the sun so long as it keeps to its lawful orbit; for he is working in harmony with the fundamental laws of the universe; he is building his life on a basis which cannot be altered or overthrown, and, therefore, all that he does will be so strong and durable, and all the parts of his life will be so coherent, harmonious, and firmly knit that it cannot possibly be brought to ruin.

### The Perfect Life

In all the universal forms which are built up by the Great Invisible and unerring Power, it will be found that the observance of mathematical law is carried out with unfailing exactitude down to the most minute detail. The microscope reveals the fact that the infinitely small is as perfect as the infinitely great.

A snowflake is as perfect as a star. Likewise, in the erection of a building by man, the strictest attention must be paid to every detail.

A foundation must first be laid, and although it is to be buried and hidden, it must receive the greatest care, and be made stronger than any other part of the building; then stone upon stone, brick upon brick is carefully laid with the aid of a plumb-line, until at last the building stands complete in its durability, strength, and beauty.

Even so it is with the life of a man. He who would have a life secure and blessed, a life freed from the miseries and failures to which so many fall victim, must carry the practice of the moral principles into every detail of his life, into every momentary duty and trivial transaction. In every little thing he must be thorough and honest, neglecting nothing.

To neglect or misapply any little detail—be he commercial man, agriculturist, professional man, or artisan—is the same as neglecting a stone or a brick in a building, and it will be a source of weakness and trouble.

The majority of those who fail and come to grief do so through neglecting the apparently *insignificant* details.

It is a common error to suppose that little things can be passed by, and that the greater things are more important, and should receive all attention; but a cursory glance at the universe, as well as a little serious reflection on life, will teach the lesson that nothing great can exist which is not made of small details, and in the composition of which every detail is perfect.

He who adopts the four ethical principles as the law and base of his life, who raises the edifice of character upon them, who in his thoughts and words and actions does not wander from them, whose every duty and every passing transaction is performed in strict accordance with their exactions—such a man, laying down the hidden foundation of integrity of heart securely and strongly, cannot fail to raise up a structure which shall bring him honor; and he is building a temple in which he can repose in peace and blessedness—even the strong and beautiful Temple of his life.

# Cultivation
of Concentration

ONCENTRATION, OR THE BRINGING of the mind to a center and keeping it there, is vitally necessary to the accomplishment of any task. It is the father of thoroughness and the mother of excellence. As a faculty, it is not an end in itself, but is an aid to all faculties, all work. Not a purpose in itself, it is yet a power which serves all purposes. Like steam in mechanics, it is a dynamic force in the machinery of the mind and the functions of life.

The faculty is a common possession, though in its perfection it is rare—just as *will* and *reason* are common possessions, though a perfectly poised will and a comprehensive reason are rare possessions—and the mystery which some modern mystical writers have thrown around it is entirely superfluous. Every successful man, in whatever direction his success may lie, practices concentration, though he may know nothing about it as a subject of study: every time one becomes absorbed in a book or task, or is rapt in devotion or assiduous in duty, concentration, in a greater or lesser degree, is brought into play.

Many books purporting to give instructions on concentration make its practice and acquisition an end in itself. There is no surer nor swifter way to destruction. The fixing of the eyes upon the tip of the nose, upon a door-knob, a picture, a mystical symbol, or the portrait of a saint; or the centering of the mind upon the navel, the pineal gland, or some imaginary point in space (I have seen all these methods seriously advised in works on this subject) with the object of acquiring concentration, is like trying to nourish the body by merely moving the jaw as in the act of eating, without taking food. Such methods prevent the end at which they aim. They lead towards dispersion and not concentration; towards weakness and imbecility rather than towards power and intelligence. I have met those who squandered, by these practices, what measure of concentration they at first possessed, and have become the prey of a weak and wandering mind.

Concentration is an aid to the doing of something; it is not the doing of something in itself. A ladder has no value in and of itself, but only insofar as it enables us to *reach* something which we could not otherwise reach. In like manner, concentration is that which enables the mind to accomplish with ease that which it would be otherwise impossible to accomplish; but of itself it is a dead thing, and not a living accomplishment.

Concentration is so interwoven with the uses of life that it cannot be separated from duty; and he who tries to acquire it *apart from his task, his duty*, will not only fail, but will diminish, and not increase, his mental control and executive capacity, and so render himself less and less fit to succeed in his undertakings.

In the task of the hour is all the means for the cultivation of concentration—whether that task be the acquiring of divine knowledge, or the sweeping of a floor—without resorting to methods which have no practical bearing on life; for what is concentration but the bringing of a well-controlled mind to the doing of that which has to be done?

### The Enemy of Concentration

He who does his work in an aimless, a hurried, or

thoughtless manner, and resorts to his artificial "concentration methods"—to his door-knob, his picture or nasal extremity—in order to gain that which he imagines to be some kind of mystical power—but which is a very ordinary and practical quality—though he may drift towards insanity (and I knew one man who became insane by these practices), he will not increase in steadiness of mind.

The great enemy of concentration—and therefore of all skill and power—is a wavering, wandering, undisciplined mind; and it is in overcoming this that concentration is acquired. A scattered and undisciplined army would be useless. To make it effective in action and swift in victory it must be solidly concentrated and masterfully directed. Scattered and diffused thoughts are weak and worthless. Thoughts marshalled, commanded, and directed upon a given point, are invincible; confusion, doubt and difficulty give way before their masterly approach. Concentrated thought enters largely into all successes, and informs all victories.

There is no more secret about its acquirement than about any other acquisition, for it is governed by the underlying principle of all development, namely, *practice*. To be able to do a thing, you must begin to *do it*, and keep on doing it until the thing is mastered.

This principle prevails universally—in all arts, sciences, trades; in all learning, conduct, religion. To be able to paint, one must paint; to know how to use a tool skillfully, he must use the tool; to become learned, he must learn; to become wise, he must do wise things; and to successfully concentrate his mind, he must concentrate it. But the doing is not all—*it must be done with energy and intelligence.*

## Concentrate on Your Work

The beginning of concentration, then, is to go to your daily task and put your mind on it, bringing all your intelligence and mental energy to a focus upon that which has to be done; and every time the thoughts are found wandering aimlessly away, they should be brought promptly back to the thing in hand. Thus the "center" upon which you are to bring your mind to a point, is (not your pineal gland or a point in space), but the work which you are doing every day; and your object in thus concentrating is to be able to do your work with smooth rapidity and consummate skill; for until you can thus do your work, you have not gained any degree of control over your mind; you have not acquired the power of concentration.

This powerful focusing of one's thought and energy and will upon the doing of things is difficult at first—as everything worth acquiring is difficult—but daily effort, strenuously made and patiently followed up, will soon lead to such a measure of self-control as will enable one to bring a strong and penetrating mind to bear upon any work undertaken; a mind that will quickly comprehend all the details of the work, and dispose of them with accuracy and despatch. He will thus, as his concentrative capacity increases enlarge his usefulness in the scheme of things, and increase his value to the world, thus inviting nobler opportunities, and opening the door to higher duties; he will also experience the joy of a wider and fuller life.

### The Four Stages of Concentration

In the process of concentration there are the four following stages:

1. **Attention**
2. **Contemplation**
3. **Abstraction**
4. **Activity in Repose**

At first the thoughts are arrested, and the mind is fixed upon the object of concentration, which is the task in hand—this is *attention*.

The mind is then roused into vigorous thought concerning the way of proceeding with the task—this is *contemplation*.

Protracted contemplation leads to a condition of mind in which the doors of the senses are all closed against the entrance of outside distractions, the thoughts being wrapped in, and solely and intensely centered upon, the work in hand—this is *abstraction*.

The mind thus centered in profound thought reaches a state in which the maximum of work is accomplished with the minimum of friction—this is *activity in repose*.

*Attention* is the first stage in all successful work. They who lack it fail in everything. Such are the lazy, the thoughtless, the indifferent and incompetent. When attention is followed by an awakening of the mind to serious thought, then the second stage is reached. To insure success in all ordinary, worldly undertakings, it is not necessary to go beyond these two stages.

They are reached, in a greater or lesser degree, by all that large army of skilled and competent workers which carries out the work of the world in its manifold departments, and only a comparatively small number reach the third stage of *abstraction*; for when abstraction is reached, we have entered the sphere of genius.

In the first two stages, the work and the mind are separate, and the work is done more or less laboriously and with a degree of friction; but in the third stage, a marriage of the work with the mind takes place, there is a fusion, a union, and the two become one; then there is a superior efficiency with less labor and friction.

In the perfection of the first two stages, the mind is objectively engaged, and is easily drawn from its center by external sights and sounds; but when the mind has attained perfection in abstraction, the *subjective* method of working is accomplished, as distinguished from the *objective*. The thinker is then oblivious to the outside world, but is vividly alive in his mental operations.

If spoken to, he will not hear, and if plied with more vigorous appeals, he will bring back his mind to outside things as one coming out of a dream; indeed, this abstraction is a kind of waking dream, but its similarity to a dream ends with the subjective state: it does not prevail in the mental operations of that state, in which, instead of the confusion of dreaming, there is a perfect order, penetrating insight, and a wide range of comprehension.

Whoever attains to perfection in abstraction will manifest genius in the particular work upon which his mind is centered. Inventors, artists, poets, scientists, philosophers, and all men of genius, are men of abstraction. They accomplish subjectively, and with ease, that which the objective workers—men who have not yet attained beyond the second stage in concentration—cannot accomplish with the most strenuous labor.

When the fourth stage—that of *activity in repose*—is attained, then concentration in its perfection is acquired. I am unable to find a single word which will fully express this dual condition of intense activity combined with steadiness, or rest, and have therefore employed the term "activity in repose."

The term appears contradictory, but the simple illustration of a spinning top will serve to explain the paradox. When a top spins at the maximum velocity, the friction is reduced to the minimum, and the top assumes that condition of perfect repose which is a sight so beautiful to the eye, and so captivating to the mind, of the schoolboy, who then says his top is "asleep." The top is apparently motionless, but it is the rest, not of inertia, but of intense and perfectly balanced activity.

So the mind that has acquired perfect concentration is, when engaged in that intense activity of thought which results in productive work of the highest kind, in a state of quiet poise and calm repose. Externally, there is no apparent activity, no disturbance, and the face of a man who has acquired this power will assume a more or less radiant calmness, and the face will be more sublimely calm when the mind is most intensely engaged in active thought.

## *The Intelligent Doer*

Each stage of concentration has its particular power. Thus the first stage, when perfected, leads to usefulness; the second leads to skill, ability, talent; the third leads to originality and genius; while the fourth leads to mastery and power, and makes leaders and teachers of men.

In the development of concentration, also, as in all objects of growth, the following stages embody the preceding ones in their entirety. Thus in contemplation, attention is contained; in abstraction, both attention and contemplation are embodied; and he who has reached the last stage, brings into play, in the act of contemplation, all four stages.

He who has perfected himself in concentration is able, at any moment, to bring his thoughts to a point upon any matter, and to search into it with the strong light of an active comprehension. He can both take a thing up and lay it down with equal deliberation. He has learned how to use his thinking faculties to fixed purposes, and guide them towards definite ends. He is an intelligent doer of things, and not a weak wanderer amid chaotic thought.

Decision, energy, alertness, as well as deliberation, judgement, and gravity, accompany the habit of concentration; and that vigorous mental training which its cultivation involves, leads, through ever-increasing usefulness and success in worldly occupations, towards that higher form of concentration called "meditation," in which the mind becomes divinely illumined, and acquires the heavenly knowledge.

# Practice of Meditation

WHEN ASPIRATION is united to *concentration*, the result is *meditation*. When a man intensely desires to reach and realize a higher, purer, and more radiant life than the merely worldly and pleasure-loving life, he engages in *aspiration*; and when he earnestly concentrates his thoughts upon the finding of that life, he practices meditation.

Without intense aspiration, there can be no meditation. Lethargy and indifference are fatal to its practice. The more intense the nature of a man, the more readily will he find meditation, and the more successfully will he practice it. A fiery nature will most rapidly scale the heights of Truth in meditation, when its aspirations have become sufficiently awakened.

Concentration is necessary to worldly success: meditation is necessary to spiritual success. Worldly skill and knowledge are acquired by concentration: spiritual skill and knowledge are acquired by meditation. By concentration a man can scale the highest heights of genius, but he cannot scale the heavenly heights of Truth: to accomplish this, he must meditate.

By concentration a man may acquire the wonderful comprehension and vast power of a Caesar; by meditation he may reach the divine wisdom and perfect peace of a Buddha. The perfection of concentration is *power*; the perfection of meditation is *wisdom*. By concentration, men acquire skill in the doing of the things of life—in science, art, trade, etc.—but by meditation, they acquire skill in *life* itself; in right living, enlightenment, wisdom, etc. Saints, sages, saviors—wise men and divine teachers—are the finished products of holy meditation.

### Meditation is Spiritual Concentration

The four stages in concentration are brought into play in meditation; the difference between the two powers being one of *direction*, and not of nature. Meditation is therefore *spiritual concentration*; the bringing of the mind to a focus in its search for the divine knowledge; the divine life; the intense dwelling, in thought, on Truth.

Thus, a man aspires to know and realize, above

all things else, the Truth; he then gives his *attention* to conduct, to life, to self-purification: giving attention to these things, he passes into serious *contemplation* of the facts, problems, and mystery of life: thus contemplating, he comes to the Truth, so fully and intensely as to become wholly absorbed in it, the mind is drawn away from its wanderings in a multitude of desires, and, solving one by one the problems of life, realizes that profound union with Truth which is the state of *abstraction*; and thus absorbed in Truth, there is a balance and poise of character, that divine *action in repose*, which is the abiding calm and peace of an emancipated and enlightened mind.

Meditation is more difficult to practice than concentration because it involves a much more severe self-discipline than that which occurs in concentration. A man can practice concentration without purifying his heart and life, whereas the process of purification is inseparable from meditation.

The object of meditation is divine enlightenment, the attainment of Truth, and is therefore interwoven with practical purity and righteousness. Thus while, at first, the time spent in actual meditation is short— perhaps only a half-hour in the early morning—the knowledge gained in that half-hour of vivid aspiration and concentrated thought is embodied in practice during the whole day. In meditation, therefore, the entire life of a man is involved; and as he advances in its practice he becomes more and more fitted to perform the duties of life in the circumstances in which he may be placed, for he becomes stronger, holier, calmer, and wiser.

## *Meditation Purifies Thought*

The principle of meditation is two-fold, namely—

1. Purification of the heart by repetitive thought on pure things.
2. Attainment of divine knowledge by embodying such purity in practical life.

Man is a *thought-being*, and his life and character are determined by the thoughts in which he habitually dwells. By practice, association, and habit, thoughts tend to repeat themselves with greater and greater ease and frequency, and so "fix" the character in a given direction by producing that automatic action which is called "habit."

By daily dwelling upon pure thoughts, the man of meditation forms the habit of pure and enlightened thinking which leads to pure and enlightened actions and well-performed duties. By the ceaseless repetition of pure thoughts, he at last becomes one with those thoughts, and is a purified being, manifesting his attainment in pure actions, in a serene and wise life.

The majority of men live in a series of conflicting desires, passions, emotions, and speculations, and there are restlessness, uncertainty, and sorrow; but when a man begins to train his mind in meditation, he gradually gains control over the inward conflict by bringing his thoughts to a focus upon a central principle. In this way the old habits of impure and erroneous thought and action are broken up, and the new habits of pure and enlightened thought and action are formed; the man becomes more and more reconciled to Truth, and there is increasing harmony and insight, a growing perfection and peace.

## *Mistaking Reverie for Meditation*

A powerful and lofty aspiration towards Truth is always accompanied with a keen sense of sorrow and brevity and mystery of life, and until this condition of mind is reached, meditation is impossible. Merely musing, or whiling away the time in idle dreaming (habits to which the word meditation is frequently applied), are very far removed from meditation, in the lofty spiritual sense which we attach to that condition.

It is easy to mistake *reverie* for meditation. This is a fatal error which must be avoided by one striving to meditate. The two must not be confounded. Reverie is a loose dreaming into which a man falls; meditation is a strong, purposeful thinking into which a man rises. Reverie is easy and pleasurable; meditation is at first difficult and irksome. Reverie thrives in indolence and luxury; meditation arises from strenuousness and discipline. Reverie is first alluring, then sensuous, and then sensual. Meditation is first forbidding, then profitable, and then peaceful. Reverie is dangerous; it undermines self-control. Meditation is protective; it establishes self-control.

There are certain signs by which one can know whether he is engaging in reverie or meditation.

## The indications of reverie are:

1. A desire to avoid exertion.
2. A desire to experience the pleasures of dreaming.
3. An increasing distaste for one's worldly duties.
4. A desire to shirk one's worldly responsibilities.
5. Fear of consequences.
6. A wish to get money with as little effort as possible.
7. Lack of self-control.

**The indications of meditation are:**

1. Increase of both physical and mental energy.
2. A strenuous striving after wisdom.
3. A decrease of irksomeness in the performance of duty.
4. A fixed determination to faithfully fulfill all worldly responsibilities.
5. Freedom from fear.
6. Indifference to riches.
7. Possession of self-control.

### Difficult Times to Meditate

There are certain times, places, and conditions in and under which it is impossible to meditate, others wherein meditation is rendered more accessible; and these, which should be known and carefully observed, are as follows:

### Times, Places, and Conditions in which Meditation is Impossible:

1. At, or immediately after, meals.
2. In places of pleasure.
3. In crowded places.
4. While walking rapidly.

5. While lying in bed in the morning.
6. While smoking.
7. While lying on a couch or bed for physical or mental relaxation.

## Times, Places, and Conditions in which Meditation is Difficult:

1. At night.
2. In a luxuriously furnished room.
3. While sitting on a soft, yielding seat.
4. While wearing ostentatious clothing.
5. While in company.
6. When the body is weary.
7. If the body is given too much food.

## Times, Places, and Conditions in which it is Best to Meditate:

1. Very early in the morning.
2. Immediately before meals.
3. In solitude.
4. In open air or in a plainly furnished room.
5. While sitting on a hard seat.
6  When the body is strong and vigorous.
7. When the body is modestly and plainly clothed.

It will be seen by the foregoing instructions that

ease, luxury, and indulgence (which induce reverie) render meditation difficult, and when strongly pronounced make it impossible; while strenuousness, discipline, and self-denial (which dispel reverie), make meditation comparatively easy.

The body, too, should be neither overfed nor starved; neither in rags nor flauntingly clothed. It should not be tired, but should be at the highest point of energy and strength, as the holding of the mind to a concentrated train of subtle and lofty thought requires a high degree of both physical and mental energy.

Aspiration can often best be aroused and the mind renewed in meditation, by the mental repetition of a lofty precept, a beautiful sentence or a verse of poetry. Indeed, the mind that is ready for meditation will instinctively adopt this practice. Mere mechanical repetition is worthless, and even a hindrance. The words repeated must be so applicable to one's own condition that they are dwelt upon lovingly and with concentrated devotion. In this way aspiration and concentration harmoniously combine to produce, without undue strain, the state of meditation.

All the conditions above stated are of the utmost importance in the early stages of meditation, and should be carefully noted and duly observed by all who are striving to acquire the practice; and those who faithfully follow the instructions, and who strive and persevere, will not fail to gather in, in due season, the harvest of purity, wisdom, bliss, and peace; and will surely eat of the fruits of holy meditation.

# The Power of Purpose

DISPERSION IS weakness; concentration is power. Destruction is a scattering, preservation a uniting, process. Things are useful and thoughts are powerful in the measure that their parts are strongly and intelligently concentrated. Purpose is highly concentrated thought. All the mental energies are directed at the attainment of an object, and obstacles which intervene between the thinker and the object are, one after another, broken down and overcome.

Purpose is the keystone in the temple of achievement. It binds and holds together in a complete whole that which would otherwise lie scattered and useless. Empty whims, ephemeral fancies, vague desires, and half-hearted resolutions have no place in purpose. In the sustained determination to accomplish there is an invincible power which swallows up all inferior considerations, and marches direct to victory.

All successful men are men of purpose. They hold fast to an idea, a project, a plan, and will not let it go; they cherish it, brood upon it, tend and develop it; and when assailed by difficulties, they refuse to be beguiled into surrender; indeed, the intensity of the purpose increases with the growing magnitude of the obstacles encountered.

## Who Can Resist Unshakable Purpose?

The men who have molded the destinies of humanity have been men mighty of purpose. Like the Roman laying his road, they have followed along a well-defined path, and have refused to swerve aside even when torture and death confronted them. The Great Leaders of the race are the mental road-makers, and mankind follows in the intellectual and spiritual paths which they have carved out and beaten.

Great is the power of purpose. To know how great, let a man study it in the lives of those whose influence has shaped the ends of nations and directed the destinies of the world. In an Alexander, a Caesar, or a Napoleon, we see the power of purpose when it is directed in worldly and personal channels; in a Confucius, a Buddha, or a Christ, we perceive its vaster power when its course is along heavenly and impersonal paths.

Power goes with intelligence. There are lesser and greater purposes according with degrees of intelligence. A great mind will always be great of purpose. A weak intelligence will be without purpose. A drifting mind argues a measure of undevelopment.

What can resist an unshakable purpose? What can stand against it or turn it aside? Inert matter yields to a living force, and circumstance succumbs to the power of purpose. Truly, the man of unlawful purpose will, in achieving his ends, destroy himself, but the man of good and lawful purpose cannot fail. It only needs that he daily renew the fire and energy of his fixed resolve, to consummate his object.

The weak man, who grieves because he is misunderstood, will not greatly achieve; the vain man, who steps aside from his resolve in order to please others and gain their approbation, will not highly achieve; the double-minded man, who thinks to compromise his purpose, will fail.

The man of fixed purpose who, whether misunderstandings and foul accusations, or flatteries and fair promises, rain upon him, does not yield a fraction of his resolve, is the man of excellence and achievement; of success, greatness, power.

Hindrances stimulate the man of purpose; difficulties nerve him to renewed exertion; mistakes, losses, pains, do not subdue him; and failures are steps in the ladder of success, for he is ever conscious of the certainty of final achievement.

All things at last yield to the silent, irresistible, all-conquering energy of purpose.

# The Joy of Accomplishment

JOY IS ALWAYS the accompaniment of a task successfully accomplished. An undertaking completed, or a piece of work done, always brings rest and satisfaction.

"When a man has done his duty, he is light-hearted and happy," says Emerson; and no matter how insignificant the task may appear, the doing of it faithfully and with whole-souled energy always results in cheerfulness and peace of mind.

Of all miserable men, the shirker is the most miserable. Thinking to find ease and happiness in avoiding difficult duties and necessary tasks, which require the expenditure of labor and exertion, his mind is always uneasy and disturbed, he becomes burdened with an inward sense of shame, and forfeits manliness and self-respect.

"He who will not work according to his faculty,

let him perish according to his necessity," says Carlyle; and it is a moral law that the man who avoids duty, and does not work to the full extent of his capacity, does actually perish, first in his character and last in his body and circumstances. Life and action are synonymous, and immediately a man tries to escape exertion, either physical or mental, he has commenced to decay.

On the other hand, the energetic increase in life by the full exercise of their powers, by overcoming difficulties, and by bringing to completion tasks which called for the strenuous use of mind or muscle.

How happy is a child when a school-lesson, long labored over, is mastered at last! The athlete, who has trained his body through long months or years of discipline and strain, is richly blessed in his increased health and strength; and is met with rejoicings of his friends when he carries home the prize from the field of contest. After many years of grudging toil, the heart of the scholar is gladdened with the advantages and powers which learning bestows. The businessman, grappling incessantly with difficulties and drawbacks, is amply repaid in the happy assurance of well-earned success; and the horticulturist, vigorously contending with the stubborn soil, sits down at last to eat of the fruits of his labor.

Every successful accomplishment, even in worldly things, is repaid with its own measure of joy; and in spiritual things, the joy which supervenes upon the perfection of purpose is sure, deep, and abiding. Great is the heartfelt joy (albeit ineffable) when, after innumerable and apparently unsuccessful attempts, some ingrained fault of character is at last cast out to trouble its erstwhile victim and the world no more. The striver after virtue—he who is engaged in the holy task of building up a noble character—tastes, at every step of conquest over self, a joy which does not again leave him, but which becomes an integral part of his spiritual nature.

All life is a struggle; both without and within there are conditions against which man must contend; his very existence is a series of efforts and accomplishments, and his right to remain among men as a useful unit of humanity depends upon the measure of his capacity for wrestling successfully with the elements of nature without, or with the enemies of virtue and truth within.

### The Reward of Accomplishment is Joy

It is demanded of man that he shall continue to

strive after better things, after greater perfection, after higher and still higher achievements; and in accordance with the measure of his obedience to this demand, does the angel of joy wait upon his footsteps and minister unto him; for he who is anxious to learn, eager to know, and who puts forth efforts to accomplish, finds the joy which eternally sings at the heart of the universe. First in little things, then in greater, and then in greater still, must man strive; until at last he is prepared to make the supreme effort, and strive for the accomplishment of Truth, succeeding in which, will realize the eternal joy.

The price of life is effort; the acme of effort is accomplishment; the reward of accomplishment is joy. Blessed is the man who strives against his own selfishness; he will taste in its fullness the joy of accomplishment.

BOOK
FOUR

*he Way
of Peace*

# TABLE OF CONTENTS

# The Power of Meditation

SPIRITUAL MEDITATION is the pathway to Divinity. It is the mystic ladder which reaches from earth to heaven, from error to Truth, from pain to peace. Every saint has climbed it; every sinner must sooner or later come to it, and every weary pilgrim that turns his back upon self and the world, and sets his face resolutely towards the Father's Home, must plant his feet upon the golden rounds. Without its aid you cannot grow into the divine state, the divine likeness, the divine peace, and the fadeless glories and unpolluting joys of Truth will remain hidden from you.

Meditation is the intense dwelling, in thought, upon an idea or theme, with the object of thoroughly comprehending it, and whatsoever you constantly meditate upon you will not only come to understand, but will grow more and more into its likeness, for it will become incorporated into your very being, will become, in fact, your very self. If, therefore, you constantly dwell upon that which is selfish and debasing, you will ultimately become selfish and debased. If you ceaselessly think upon that which is pure and unselfish you will surely become pure and unselfish.

Tell me what that is upon which you most frequently and intensely think, that to which, in your silent hours, your soul most naturally turns, and I will tell you to what place of pain or peace you are traveling, and whether you are growing into the likeness of the divine or the bestial.

There is an unavoidable tendency to become literally the embodiment of that quality upon which one most constantly thinks. Let, therefore, the object of your meditation be above and not below, so that every time you revert to it in thought you will be lifted up; let it be pure and unmixed with any selfish element; so shall your heart become purified and drawn nearer to Truth, and not defiled and dragged more hopelessly into error.

## The Secret of Growth is Meditation

Meditation, in the spiritual sense in which I am now using it, is the secret of all growth in spiritual life and knowledge. Every prophet, sage and savior became such by the power of meditation. Buddha meditated upon the truth until he could say, "I am the Truth." Jesus brooded upon the Divine immanence until at last he could declare, "I and my Father are One."

Meditation centered upon divine realities is the very essence and soul of prayer. It is the silent reaching of the soul toward the Eternal. Mere petitionary prayer without meditation is a body without a soul, and is powerless to lift the mind and heart above sin and affliction.

If you are daily praying for wisdom, for peace, for loftier purity and fuller realization of Truth, and that for which you pray is still far from you, it means that you are praying for one thing while living out in thought and act another.

If you will cease from such waywardness, taking your mind off those things the selfish clinging to which debars you from the possession of the stainless realities for which you pray; if you will no longer ask God to grant you that which you do not deserve, or to bestow upon you that love and compassion which you refuse to bestow upon others, but will commence to think and act in the spirit of Truth, you will day by day be growing into those realities, so that ultimately you will become one with them.

## Heavenly Gains Require Effort

He who would secure any worldly advantage must be willing to work vigorously for it, and he would be foolish indeed who, waiting with folded hands, expected it to come to him for the mere asking. Do not then vainly imagine that you can obtain the heavenly possessions without making an effort. Only when you commence to work earnestly in the Kingdom of Truth will you be allowed to partake of the Bread of Life, and when you have, by patient and uncomplaining effort, earned the spiritual wages for which you ask, they will not be withheld from you.

If you really seek Truth, and not merely your own gratification; if you love it above all earthly pleasures and gains; more, even than happiness itself, you will be willing to make the effort necessary for its achievement.

If you would be freed from sin and sorrow; if you would taste that spotless purity for which you sigh and pray; if you would enter into the possession of profound and abiding peace, come now and enter the path of meditation, and let the supreme object of your meditation be Truth.

At the outset, meditation must be distinguished from *idle reverie*. There is nothing dreamy and unpractical about it. It is a process of *searching and uncompromising thought which allows nothing to remain but the simple and naked truth*. Thus meditating you will no longer strive to build yourself up in your prejudices, but, forgetting self, you will remember only that you are seeking the Truth. And so you will remove, one by one, the errors which you have built around yourself in the past, and will patiently wait for the revelation of Truth which will come when your errors have been sufficiently removed. In the silent humility of the heart you will realize that:

> *There is an inmost center in us all*
> *Where Truth abides in fullness; and around,*
> *Wall upon wall, the gross flesh hems it in;*
> *This perfect, clear perception, which is Truth,*
> *A baffling and perverting carnal mesh*
> *Blinds it, and makes all error; and to know,*
> *Rather consists in opening out a way*
> *Whence the imprisoned splendor may escape,*
> *Than in effecting entry for a light*
> *Supposed to be without.*

### Cease Being Lazy

Select some portion of the day in which to meditate, and keep that period sacred to your purpose. The best time is the very early morning when the spirit of repose is upon everything. All natural conditions will then be in your favor; the passions, after the long bodily fast of the night, will be subdued, the excitements and worries of the previous day will have died away, and the mind, strong and yet restful, will be receptive to spiritual instruction. Indeed, one of the first efforts you will be called upon to make will be to shake off lethargy and indulgence, and if you refuse you will be unable to advance, for the demands of the spirit are imperative.

To be spiritually awakened is also to be mentally and physically awakened. The sluggard and the self-indulgent can have no knowledge of Truth. He who, possessed of health and strength, wastes the calm, precious hours of the silent morning in drowsy indulgence is totally unfit to climb the heavenly heights.

### Awakening Early

He whose awakening consciousness has become alive to its lofty possibilities, who is beginning to shake off the darkness of ignorance in which the world is enveloped, rises before the stars have ceased their vigil, and grappling with the darkness within his soul, strives, by holy aspiration, to perceive the light of Truth while the unawakened world dreams on.

*The heights by great men reached and kept,*
*Were not attained by sudden flight,*
*But they, while their companions slept,*
*Were toiling upward in the night.*

No saint, no holy man, no teacher of Truth ever lived who did not rise early in the morning. Jesus habitually rose early, and climbed the solitary mountains to engage in holy communion. Buddha always rose an hour before sunrise and engaged in meditation, and all his disciples were enjoined to do the same.

If you have to commence your daily duties at a very early hour, and are thus debarred from giving the early morning hours to systematic meditation, try to give an hour at night, and should this, by the length and laboriousness of your daily task be denied to you, you need not despair, for you may turn your thoughts upward in holy meditation in the intervals of your work, or in those few idle minutes which you now waste in aimlessness; and should your work be of the kind which becomes by practice automatic, you may meditate while engaged upon it.

The eminent Christian saint and philosopher, Jacob Boehme, realized his vast knowledge of things while working long hours as a shoemaker. In every life there is time to think, and the busiest, the most laborious is not shut out from aspiration and meditation.

### Meditation Gives Strength

Spiritual meditation and self-discipline are inseparable; you will, therefore, commence to meditate upon yourself so as to try and understand yourself. Remember, the great object you will have in view will be the complete removal of all your errors in order that you may realize Truth. You will begin to question your motives, thoughts and acts, comparing them with your ideal, and endeavoring to look upon them with a calm and impartial eye. In this manner you will be continually gaining more of that mental and spiritual equilibrium without which men are but helpless straws upon the ocean of life.

If you are given to hatred or anger, you will meditate upon gentleness and forgiveness, so as to become actually alive to a sense of your harsh and foolish conduct. You will then begin to dwell in thoughts of love, of gentleness, of abounding forgiveness; and as you overcome the lower by the higher, there will gradually, silently steal into your heart a knowledge of the Divine Law of Love with an understanding of its bearing upon all the intricacies of life and conduct.

And in applying this knowledge to your every thought, word, and act, you will grow more and more gentle, more and more loving, more and more divine. And thus with every error, every selfish desire, every human weakness; by the power of meditation is it overcome, and as each sin, each error is thrust out, a fuller and clearer measure of the Light of Truth illumines the pilgrim soul.

Thus meditating, you will be ceaselessly fortifying yourself against your only *real* enemy, your selfish, perishable self, and will be establishing yourself more and more firmly in the divine and imperishable self that is inseparable from Truth.

The direct outcome of your meditations will be a calm, spiritual strength which will be your stay and resting-place in the struggle of life. Great is the overcoming power of holy thought, and the strength and knowledge gained in the hour of silent meditation will enrich the soul with saving remembrance in the hour of strife, of sorrow, or of temptation.

As, by the power of meditation, you grow in wisdom, you will relinquish, more and more, your selfish desires which are fickle, impermanent, and productive of sorrow and pain; and will take your stand, with increasing steadfastness and trust, upon unchangeable principles, and will realize heavenly rest.

### Trust in Divine Principles

The use of meditation is the acquirement of a knowledge of eternal principles, and the power which results from meditation is the ability to rest upon and trust these principles, and so become one with the Eternal. The end of meditation is, therefore, direct knowledge of Truth, God, and the realization of divine and profound peace.

Let your meditations take their rise from the ethical ground which you now occupy. Remember that you are to *grow* into Truth by steady perseverance. If you are an orthodox Christian, meditate ceaselessly upon the spotless purity and divine excellence of the character of Jesus, and apply his every precept to your inner life and outward conduct, so as to approximate more and more toward his perfection.

Do not be as those religious ones, who, refusing

to meditate upon the Law of Truth, and to put into practice the precepts given to them by their Master, are content to formally worship, to cling to their particular creeds, and to continue in the ceaseless round of sin and suffering.

Strive to rise, by the power of meditation, above all selfish clinging to partial gods or party creeds, above dead formalities and lifeless ignorance. Thus walking the highway of wisdom, with mind fixed upon the spotless Truth, you shall know no stopping place short of the realization of Truth. He who earnestly meditates first perceives a truth, as it were, afar off, and then realizes it by daily practice. It is only the doer of the Word of Truth that can know of the doctrine of Truth, for though by pure thought the Truth is perceived, it is only actualized by practice.

### Buddha's Five Great Meditations

Said the divine Gautama, the Buddha, "He who gives himself up to vanity, and does not give himself up to meditation, forgetting the real aim of life and grasping at pleasure, will in time envy him who has exerted himself in meditation," and he instructed his disciples in the following "Five Great Meditations":

"The first meditation is the meditation of love, in

which you so adjust your heart that you long for the benefit and welfare of all beings, including the happiness of your enemies.

"The second meditation is the meditation of pity, in which you think of all beings in distress, vividly representing in your imagination their sorrows and anxieties so as to arouse a deep compassion for them in your soul.

"The third meditation is the meditation of joy, in which you think of the prosperity of others, and rejoice with their rejoicings.

"The fourth meditation is the meditation of impurity, in which you consider the evil consequences of corruption, the effects of sin and diseases. How trivial often the pleasure of the moment, and fatal its consequences.

"The fifth meditation is the meditation on serenity, in which you rise above love and hate, tyranny and oppression, wealth and want, and regard your own fate with impartial calmness and perfect tranquility."

## Have Lofty Aspirations

By engaging in these meditations the disciples of Buddha arrived at a knowledge of the Truth. But whether you engage in these particular meditations or not matters little so long as your object is Truth, so long as you hunger and thirst for that righteousness which is a holy heart and a blameless life.

In your meditations, therefore, let your heart grow and expand with ever-broadening love, until, free from all hatred, and passion, and condemnation, it embraces the whole universe with thoughtful tenderness. As the flower opens its petals to receive the morning light, so open your soul more and more to the glorious light of Truth. Soar upon the wings of aspiration; be fearless, and believe in the loftiest possibilities.

Believe that a life of absolute meekness is possible; believe that a life of stainless purity is possible; believe that a life of perfect holiness is possible; believe that the realization of the highest truth is possible. He who so believes climbs rapidly the heavenly hills, while the unbelievers continue to grope darkly and painfully in the fog-bound valleys.

So believing, so aspiring, so meditating, divinely sweet and beautiful will be your spiritual experiences, and glorious the revelations that will enrapture your inward vision. As you realize the divine Love, the divine Justice, the divine Purity, the perfect Law of Good, or God, great will be your bliss and deep your peace.

Old things will pass away, and all things will become new. The veil of the material universe, so dense and impenetrable to the eye of error, so thin and transparent to the eye of Truth, will be lifted and the spiritual universe will be revealed. Time will cease and you will live only in Eternity. Change and mortality will no more cause you anxiety and sorrow, for you become established in the unchangeable, and will dwell in the very heart of immortality.

# The Two Masters,
# Self & Truth

UPON THE BATTLEFIELD of the human soul two masters are ever contending for the crown of supremacy, for the kingship and dominion of the heart; the master of the self, called also the "Prince of this world," and the master of Truth, called also the Father God. The master self is that rebellious one whose weapons are passion, pride, avarice, vanity, self-will, implements of darkness; the master Truth is that meek and lowly one whose weapons are gentleness, patience, purity, sacrifice, humility, love, instruments of Light.

In every soul the battle is waged, and as a soldier cannot engage at once in two opposing armies, so every heart is enlisted either in the ranks of self or of Truth. There is no half-and-half course; "There is self and there is Truth; where self is, Truth is not; where

Truth is, self is not." Thus spoke Buddha, the teacher of Truth, and Jesus, the manifested Christ, declared that "No man can serve two masters; for either he will hate the one and love the other; or else he will hold to the one and despise the other. Ye cannot serve God and Mammon."

Truth is so simple, so absolutely undeviating and uncompromising that it admits of no complexity, no turning, no qualification. Self is ingenious, crooked, and, governed by subtle and snaky desire, admits of endless turnings and qualifications, and the deluded worshippers of self vainly imagine that they can gratify every worldly desire, and at the same time possess the Truth. But the lovers of Truth worship Truth with the sacrifice of self, and ceaselessly guard themselves against worldliness and self-seeking.

### Sacrifice for Truth

Do you seek to know and to realize Truth? Then you must be prepared to sacrifice, to renounce to the uttermost, for Truth in all its glory can only be perceived and known when the last vestige of self has disappeared.

The eternal Christ declared that he who would be His disciple must "deny himself daily." Are you willing to deny yourself, to give up your lusts, your prejudices, your opinions? If so, you may enter the narrow way of Truth, and find that peace from which the world is shut out. The absolute denial, the utter extinction, of self is the perfect state of Truth, and all religions and philosophies are but so many aids to this supreme attainment.

Self is the denial of Truth. Truth is the denial of self. As you let self die, you will be reborn in Truth. As you cling to self, Truth will be hidden from you.

When you cling to self, your path will be beset with difficulties, and repeated pains, sorrows and disappointments will be your lot. There are no difficulties in Truth, and coming to Truth, you will be freed from all sorrow and disappointment.

Truth in itself is not hidden and dark. It is always revealed and is perfectly transparent. But the blind and wayward self cannot perceive it. The light of day is not hidden except to the blind, and the light of Truth is not hidden except to those who are blinded by self.

Truth is the one reality in the universe, the inward harmony, the perfect justice, the eternal Love. Nothing can be added to it, nor taken from it. It does not depend upon any man, but all men depend upon it.

You cannot perceive the beauty of Truth while you are looking out through the eyes of self. If you are vain, you will color everything with your own vanities. If lustful, your heart and mind will be so clouded with the smoke and flames of passion, that everything will appear distorted through them. If proud and opinionated, you will see nothing in the whole universe except the magnitude and importance of your own opinions.

There is one quality which preeminently distinguishes the man of Truth from the man of self, and that is *humility*. To be not only free from vanity, stubbornness and egotism, but to regard one's own opinions as of no value, this indeed is true humility.

### Truth is the One True Religion

He who is immersed in self regards his own opinions as Truth, and the opinions of other men as error. But that humble Truth-lover who has learned to distinguish between opinion and Truth, regards all men with the eye of charity, and does not seek to defend his opinions against theirs, but sacrifices those opinions that he may love the more, that he may manifest the spirit of Truth, for Truth in its very nature is inexpressible and can only be lived. He who has the most of charity has most of Truth.

Men engage in heated controversies, and foolishly imagine they are defending the Truth, when in reality they are merely defending their own petty interests and perishable opinions. The follower of self takes up arms against others. The follower of Truth takes up arms against himself. Truth, being unchangeable and eternal, is independent of your opinion and of mine. We may both enter into it, or we may stay outside; but both our defense and our attack is superfluous, and are hurled back upon ourselves.

Men, enslaved by self, passionate, proud, and condemnatory, believe their particular creed or religion to be the Truth, and all other religions in error; and they proselytize with passionate ardor. There is but one religion, the religion of Truth. There is but one error, the error of self. Truth is not a formal belief; it is an unselfish, holy and aspiring heart, and he who has Truth is at peace with all, and cherishes all with thoughts of love.

You may easily know whether you are a child of Truth or a worshipper of self, if you will silently examine your mind, heart, and conduct. Do you harbor thoughts of suspicion, enmity, envy, lust, pride or do you strenuously fight against these? If the former, you are chained to self, no matter what religion you may profess; if the latter, you are a candidate for Truth, even though outwardly you may possess no religion.

Are you passionate, self-willed, ever seeking to gain your own ends, self-indulgent, and self-centered; or are you gentle, mild, unselfish, quit of every form of self-indulgence, and are ever ready to give up your own? If the former, self is your master; if the latter, Truth is the object of your affection.

Do you strive for riches? Do you fight with passion for your party? Do you lust for power and leadership? Are you given to ostentation and self-praise? Or have you given up love of riches? Have you relinquished all strife? Are you content to take the lowest place, and to be passed by unnoticed? And have you ceased to talk about yourself and to regard yourself with complacent pride? If the former, even though you may imagine you worship God, the god of your heart is self. If the latter, even though you may withhold your lips from worship, you are dwelling with the Most High.

The signs by which the Truth-lover is known are unmistakable. Hear the Holy Krishna declare them, in Sir Edwin Arnold's beautiful rendering of the "Bhagavad Gita":

*Fearlessness, singleness of soul, the will*
*Always to strive for wisdom; opened hand*
*And governed appetites; and piety,*
*And love of lonely study, humbleness,*
*Uprightness, heed to injure nought which lives,*
*Truthfulness, slowness unto wrath, a mind*
*That lightly letteth go what others prize;*
*And equanimity, and charity*
*Which spieth no man's faults; and tenderness*
*Towards all that suffer; a contented heart,*
*Fluttered by no desires; a bearing mild,*
*Modest and grave, with manhood nobly mixed,*
*With patience, fortitude and purity;*
*An unrevengeful spirit, never given*
*To rate itself too high—such be the signs,*
*O Indian Prince! Of him whose feet are set*
*On that fair path which leads to heavenly birth!*

When men, lost in the devious ways of error and self, have forgotten the "heavenly birth," the state of holiness and Truth, they set up artificial standards by which to judge one another, and make acceptance of, and adherence to, their own particular theology, the test of Truth; and so men are divided one against the other, and there is ceaseless enmity and strife, and unending sorrow and suffering.

## *Allow the Self to Die*

Reader, do you seek to realize the birth into Truth? There is only one way: *Let self die.* All those lusts, appetites, desires, opinions, limited conceptions and prejudices to which you have hitherto so tenaciously clung, let them fall from you. Let them no longer hold you in bondage, and Truth will be yours. Cease to look upon your own religion as superior to all others, and strive humbly to learn the supreme lesson of charity.

No longer cling to the idea so productive of strife and sorrow, that the Savior whom you worship is the only Savior, and that the Savior whom your brother worships with equal sincerity and ardor, is an imposter; but seek diligently the path of holiness, and then you will realize that every holy man is a savior of mankind.

The giving-up of self is not merely the renunciation of outward things. It consists of the renunciation of the inward sin, the inward error. Not by giving up vain clothing; not by relinquishing riches, not by abstaining from certain foods; not by speaking smooth words; not by merely doing these things is the Truth found; but by giving up the spirit of vanity; by relinquishing the desire for riches; by abstaining from the lust of self-indulgence; by giving up all hatred, strife, condemnation, and self-seeking, and becoming gentle and pure at heart; by doing these things is the Truth found. To do the former, and not to do the latter, is pharisaism and hypocrisy, whereas the latter includes the former.

You may renounce the outward world, and isolate yourself in a cave or in the depths of a forest, but you will take all your selfishness with you, and unless you renounce that, great indeed will be your wretchedness and deep your delusion. You may remain just where you are, performing all your duties, and yet renounce the world, the inward enemy. To be in the world and yet not of the world is the highest perfection, the most blessed peace, is to achieve the greatest victory. The renunciation of self is the way of Truth, therefore,

*Enter the Path; there is no grief like hate,*
*No pain like passion, no deceit like sense;*
*Enter the Path; far hath he gone whose foot*
*Treads down one fond offense.*

## The Simplicity of Truth

As you succeed in overcoming self you will begin to see things in their right relations. He who is swayed by any passion, prejudice, like or dislike, adjusts everything to that particular bias, and sees only his own delusions.

He who is absolutely free from all passion, prejudice, preference, and partiality, sees himself as he is; sees others as they are; sees all things in their proper proportions and right relations. Having nothing to attack, nothing to defend, nothing to conceal, and no interests to guard, he is at peace. He has realized the profound simplicity of Truth, for this unbiased, tranquil, blessed state of mind and heart is the state of Truth. He who attains to it dwells with the angels, and sits at the footstool of the Supreme.

Knowing the Great Law; knowing the origin of sorrow; knowing the secret of suffering; knowing the way of emancipation in Truth, how can such a one engage in strife or condemnation; for though he knows that the blind, self-seeking world, surrounded with the clouds of its own illusions, and enveloped in the darkness of error and self, cannot perceive the steadfast Light of Truth, and is utterly incapable of comprehending the profound simplicity of the heart that has died, or is dying, to self. Yet he also knows that when the suffering ages have piled up mountains of sorrow, the crushed and burdened soul of the world will fly to its final refuge. When the ages are completed, every prodigal will come back to the fold of Truth. And so he dwells in goodwill towards all, and regards all with that tender compassion which a father bestows upon his wayward children.

Men cannot understand Truth because they cling to self, because they believe in and love self, because they believe self to be the only reality, whereas it is the one delusion.

When you cease to believe in and love self you will desert it, and will fly to Truth, and will find the Eternal Reality.

### All Suffering Ends in Truth

When men are intoxicated with the wines of luxury, and pleasure, and vanity, the thirst of life grows and deepens within them, and they delude themselves with dreams of fleshly immortality, but when they come to reap the harvest of their own sowing, and pain and sorrow supervene, then, crushed and humiliated, relinquishing self and all the intoxications of self, they come, with aching hearts to the one immortality, the immortality that destroys all delusions, the spiritual immortality in Truth.

Men pass from evil to good, from self to Truth,

through the dark gate of sorrow, for sorrow and self are inseparable. Only in the peace and bliss of Truth is all sorrow vanquished. If you suffer disappointment because your cherished plans have been thwarted, or because someone has not come up to your anticipations, it is because you are clinging to self. If you suffer remorse for your conduct, it is because you are clinging to self. If you are overwhelmed with chagrin and regret because of the attitude of someone else toward you, it is because you have been cherishing self. If you are wounded on account of what has been done to you or said to you, it is because you are walking in the painful way of self.

All suffering is of self. All suffering ends in Truth. When you have entered into and realized Truth, you will no longer suffer disappointment, remorse and regret, and sorrow will flee from you.

> *Self is the only prison that can ever bind the soul;*
> *Truth is the only angel that can bid the gates unroll;*
> *And when he comes to call thee,*
> *arise and follow fast;*
> *His way may lie through darkness,*
> *but it leads to light at last.*

The woe of the world is of its own making. Sorrow purifies and deepens the soul, and the extremity of sorrow is the prelude to Truth.

Have you suffered much? Have you sorrowed deeply? Have you pondered seriously upon the problem of life? If so, you are prepared to wage war against the self, and to become a disciple of Truth.

The intellectuals who do not see the necessity for giving up self, frame endless theories about the universe, and call them Truth; but if you pursue that direct line of conduct which is the practice of righteousness, you will realize the Truth which has no place in theory, and which never changes. Cultivate your heart. Water it continually with unselfish love and deep-felt pity, and strive to shut out from it all thoughts and feelings which are not in accordance with Love. Return good for evil, love for hatred, gentleness for ill-treatment, and remain silent when attacked. So shall you transmute all your selfish desires into the pure gold of Love, and self will disappear in Truth. So will you walk blamelessly among men, yoked with the easy yoke of lowliness, and clothed with the divine garment of humility.

# Acquiring
# Spiritual Power

THE WORLD IS FILLED with men and women seeking pleasure, excitement, novelty; seeking ever to be moved to laughter or tears; not seeking strength, stability, and power; but courting weakness, and eagerly engaged in dispersing what power they have.

Men and women of real power and influence are few, because few are prepared to make the sacrifice necessary to acquire power and fewer still are ready to patiently build up character.

To be swayed by your fluctuating thoughts and impulses is to be weak and powerless; to rightly control and direct these forces is to be strong and powerful. Men of strong animal passions have much of the ferocity of the beast, but this is not power. The elements of power are there; but it is only when this ferocity is tamed and subdued by the higher intelligence that real power begins; and men can only grow in power by awakening themselves to higher and ever higher states of intelligence and consciousness.

The difference between a man of weakness and one of power lies not in the strength of the personal will (for the stubborn man is usually weak and foolish), but in that focus of consciousness which represents their states of knowledge.

The pleasure seekers, the lovers of excitement, the hunters after novelty and the victims of impulse and hysterical emotion lack that knowledge of principles which gives balance, stability and influence.

### The Work That Endures

A man commences to develop power when, checking his impulses and selfish inclinations, he falls back upon the higher and calmer consciousness within him, and begins to steady himself upon a principle.

The realization of unchanging principles in consciousness is at once the source and secret of the highest power.

When, after much searching, and suffering, and sacrificing, the light of an eternal principle dawns upon the soul, a divine calm ensues and joy unspeakable gladdens the heart.

He who has realized such a principle ceases to wander, and remains poised and self-possessed. He ceases to be "passion's slave," and becomes a master-builder in the Temple of Destiny.

The man that is governed by self, and not by a principle, changes his front when his selfish comforts are threatened. Deeply intent upon defending and guarding his own interests, he regards all means as lawful that will subserve that end. He is continually scheming as to how he may protect himself against his enemies, being too self-centered to perceive that he is his own enemy. Such a man's work crumbles away, for it is divorced from Truth and power. All effort that is grounded upon self, perishes; only that work endures that is built upon an indestructible principle.

## Do Not Desert Your Principles

The man that stands upon a principle is the same calm, dauntless, self-possessed man under all circumstances. When the hour of trial comes, and he has to decide between his personal comforts and Truth, he gives up his comforts and remains firm. Even the prospect of torture and death cannot alter or deter him. The man of self regards the loss of his wealth, his comforts, or his life as the greatest of calamities which can befall him. The man of principle looks upon these incidents as comparatively insignificant, and not to be weighed with loss of character, loss of Truth. To desert Truth is, to him, the only happening which can be called a calamity.

It is the hour of crisis which decides who are the minions of darkness, and who the children of light. It is the epoch of threatening disasters, ruin, and persecution which divides the sheep from the goats, and reveals to the reverential gaze of succeeding ages the men and women of power.

It is easy for a man, so long as he is left in the enjoyment of his possessions, to persuade himself that he believes in and adheres to the principles of Peace, Brotherhood, and Universal Love; but if, when his enjoyments are threatened, or he imagines they are threatened, he begins to clamor loudly for war, he shows that he believes in and stands upon, not Peace, Brotherhood, and Love, but strife, selfishness and hatred.

He who does not desert his principles when threatened with the loss of every earthly thing, even to the loss of reputation and life, is the man of power; is the man whose every word and work endures; is the man whom the afterworld honors, reveres, and worships. Rather than desert that principle of Divine Love on which he rested, Jesus endured the utmost extremity of agony and deprivation; and today the world prostrates itself at his pierced feet in rapt adoration.

### Realization of a Principle Confers Power

There is no way to the acquiring of spiritual power except by that inward illumination and enlightenment which is the realization of spiritual principles; and those principles can be realized by constant practice and application.

Take the principle of divine Love, and quietly meditate upon it with the object of arriving at a thorough understanding of it. Bring its searching light to bear upon all your habits, your actions, your communication with others, your every secret thought and desire. As you persevere in this course, the divine Love will become more and more perfectly revealed to you, and your own shortcomings will stand out in more and more vivid contrast, spurring you on to renewed endeavor; and having once caught a glimpse of that imperishable principle, you will never again rest in your weakness, your selfishness, your imperfection, but will pursue that Love until you have relinquished every discordant element, and have brought yourself into perfect harmony with it. And that state of inward harmony is spiritual power.

Take also other spiritual principles, such as Purity and Compassion, and apply them in the same way, and so exacting is Truth, you will be able to make no stay, no resting-place until the inmost garment of your soul is devoid of every stain, and your heart has become incapable of any hard, condemnatory, and pitiless impulse.

Only insofar as you understand, realize and rely upon these principles, will you acquire spiritual power, and that power will be manifested in and through you in the form of increasing dispassion, patience and equanimity.

### The Way of Power

Dispassion argues superior self-control; sublime patience is the very hallmark of divine knowledge, and to retain an unbroken calm amid all the duties and distractions of life, marks the man of power. *It is easy in the world to live after the world's opinion; it is easy in solitude to live after our own; but the great man is he who in the midst of the crowd keeps with perfect sweetness the independence of solitude.*

Some mystics hold that perfection in dispassion is the source of that power by which miracles (so-called) are performed, and truly he who has gained such perfect control of all his interior forces that no shock, however great, can for one moment unbalance him, must be capable of guiding and directing those forces with a master-hand.

To grow in self-control, in patience, in equanimity, is to grow in strength and power; and you can only thus grow by focusing your consciousness upon a principle. As a child, after making many and vigorous attempts to walk unaided, at last succeeds, after numerous falls, in accomplishing this, so you must enter the way of power by first attempting to stand alone. Break away from the tyranny of custom, tradition, conventionality, and the opinions of others, until you succeed in walking lonely and erect amongst men.

Rely upon your own judgement; be true to your own conscience; follow the Light that is within you; all outward lights are so many will-o'-the-wisps. There will be those who tell you that you are foolish; that your judgement is faulty; that your conscience is all awry, and that the Light within you is darkness; but heed them not. If what they say is true, the sooner you, as a searcher of wisdom, find it out the better, and you can only make that discovery by bringing your powers to the test. Therefore, pursue your course bravely.

### Defying the Storm

Your conscience is at least your own, and to follow it is to be courageous; to follow the conscience of another is to be a slave. You will have many falls, will suffer many wounds, will endure many buffetings for a time, but press on in faith, believing that sure and certain victory lies ahead.

Search for a rock, a principle, and having found it cling to it; get it under your feet, and stand erect upon it, until at last, immovably fixed upon it, you succeed in defying the fury of the waves and storms of selfishness.

For selfishness in any and every form is dissipation, weakness, death; unselfishness in its spiritual aspect is conservation, power, life. As you grow in spiritual life, and become established upon principles, you will become as beautiful and as unchangeable as those principles, will taste of the

sweetness of their immortal essence, and will realize the eternal and indestructible nature of the
God within.

# The Realization
# of Selfless Love

IT IS SAID THAT MICHELANGELO saw in every rough block of stone a thing of beauty awaiting the master-hand to bring it into reality. Even so, within each there reposes the divine Image awaiting the master-hand of Faith and the chisel of Patience to bring it into manifestation. And that divine Image is revealed and realized as stainless, selfless Love.

Hidden deep in every human heart, though frequently covered up with a mass of hard and almost impenetrable accretions, is the spirit of divine Love, whose holy and spotless essence is undying and eternal. It is the Truth in man; it is that which belongs to the Supreme: that which is real and immortal. All else changes and passes away; this alone is permanent and imperishable and to realize this Love by ceaseless diligence in the practice of the highest righteousness, to live in it and to become fully conscious in it, is to enter into immortality here and now, is to become one with Truth, one with God, one with the central Heart of all things, and to know our own divine and eternal nature.

To reach this Love, to understand and experience it, one must work with great persistency and diligence upon his heart and mind, must ever renew his patience and keep strong his faith, for there will be much to remove, much to accomplish, before the divine image is revealed in all its glorious beauty.

### *Failure is an Illusion*

He who strives to reach and to accomplish the divine will be tried to the very uttermost; and this is absolutely necessary, for how else could one acquire that sublime patience without which there is no real wisdom, no divinity? Now and then, as he proceeds, all his work will seem to be futile, and his efforts appear to be thrown away. Now and then a hasty touch will mar his image, and perhaps when he imagines his work is almost completed he will find what he imagines to be the beautiful form of Divine Love utterly destroyed, and he must begin again with his past bitter experience to guide and help him. But he who has resolutely set himself to realize the Highest recognizes there is no such thing as defeat.

All failures are apparent, not real. Every slip, every fall, every return to selfishness is a lesson learned, an experience gained, from which a golden grain of wisdom is extracted, helping the striver toward the accomplishment of his lofty object. To recognize:

> *That of our vices we can frame*
> *A ladder if we will but tread*
> *Beneath our feet each deed of shame,*

is to enter the way that leads unmistakably towards the Divine, and the failings of one who thus recognizes are so many dead selves, upon which he rises, as upon stepping stones, to higher things.

### Human Love and Divine Love

Once you come to regard your failings, your sorrows and sufferings as so many voices telling you plainly where you are weak and faulty, where you fall below the true and the divine, you will then begin to ceaselessly watch yourself, and every slip, every pang of pain will show you where you are to set to work, and what you have to remove out of your heart in order to bring it nearer to the likeness of the Divine, nearer to the Perfect Love. And as you proceed, day by day detaching yourself more and more from the inward selfishness, the Love that is selfless will gradually become revealed to you.

And when you are growing patient and calm, when your petulances, tempers, and irritabilities are passing away from you, and the more powerful lusts and prejudices cease to dominate and enslave you, then you will know that the divine is awakening within you, that you are not far from that selfless Love, the possession of which is peace and immortality.

Divine Love is distinguished from human loves in this supremely important particular: *it is free from partiality*. Human loves cling to a particular object to the exclusion of all else, and when the object is removed, great and deep is the resultant suffering to the one who loves. Divine Love embraces the whole universe, and, without clinging to any part, yet contains within itself the whole, and he who comes to it by gradually purifying and broadening his human loves until all the selfish and impure elements are burnt out of them, ceases from suffering.

It is because human loves are narrow and confined and mingled with selfishness that they cause suffering. No suffering can result from that Love which is so absolutely pure that it seeks nothing for itself. Nevertheless, human loves are absolutely necessary as steps toward the Divine, and no soul is prepared to partake of Divine Love until it has become capable of the deepest and most intense human love. It is only by passing through human loves and human sufferings that Divine Love is reached and realized.

All human loves are perishable like the forms to which they cling; but there is a Love that is imperishable, and that does not cling to appearances.

All human loves are counterbalanced by human hates; but there is a Love that admits of no opposite or reaction; divine and free from all taint of self, that sheds its fragrance on all alike.

Human loves are reflections of the Divine Love, and draw the soul nearer to the reality, the Love that knows neither sorrow nor change.

### We Learn by Suffering

It is understandable that the mother, clinging with passionate tenderness to the helpless form of flesh that lies on her bosom, should be overwhelmed with the dark waters of sorrow when she sees her child laid in the cold earth. It is understandable that her tears should flow and her heart ache, for only thus can she be reminded of the fleeting nature of the joys and objects of sense, and be drawn nearer to the eternal and imperishable Reality.

It is understandable that lover, brother, sister, husband, wife should suffer deep anguish, and be enveloped in gloom when the visible object of their affections is torn from them, so that they may learn to turn their affections toward the invisible Source of all, where alone abiding satisfaction is to be found.

It is understandable that the proud, the ambitious, the self-seeking, should suffer defeat, humiliation, and misfortune; that they should pass through the scorching fires of affliction; for only thus can the wayward soul be brought to reflect upon the enigma of life; only thus can the heart be softened and purified, and prepared to receive the Truth.

When the sting of anguish penetrates the heart of human love; when gloom and loneliness and desertion cloud the soul of friendship and trust, then it is that the heart turns toward the sheltering love of the Eternal, and finds rest in its silent peace. And whatsoever comes to this Love is not turned away comfortless, is not pierced with anguish nor surrounded with gloom; and is never deserted in the dark hour of trial.

### Divine Love Seeks No Reward

The glory of divine Love can only be revealed in the heart that is chastened by sorrow, and the image of the heavenly state can only be perceived and realized when the lifeless, formless accretions of ignorance and self are hewn away.

Only that Love that seeks no personal gratification or reward, that does not make distinctions, and that leaves behind no heartaches, can be called divine.

Men, clinging to self and the comfortless shadows of evil, are in the habit of thinking of divine Love as something belonging to God who is out of reach; as something outside themselves, and that must forever remain outside. Truly, the Love of God is ever beyond the reach of self, but when the heart and mind are emptied of self then the selfless Love, the supreme Love, the Love that is of God or Good becomes an inward and abiding reality.

And this inward realization of holy Love is none other than the Love of Christ that is so much talked about and so little comprehended. The Love that not only saves the soul from sin, but lifts it also above the power of temptation.

## *The Love of Christ*

But how may one attain this sublime realization? The answer which Truth has always given, and will ever give to this question is, "Empty thyself, and I will fill thee." Divine Love cannot be known until self is dead, for self is the denial of Love, and how can that which is known be also denied? Not until the stone of self is rolled away from the sepulchre of the soul does the immortal Christ, the pure Spirit of Love, hitherto crucified, dead and buried, cast off the bonds of ignorance, and come forth in all the majesty of His resurrection.

You believe that the Christ of Nazareth was put to death and rose again. I do not say you err in that belief; but if you refuse to believe that the gentle spirit of Love is crucified daily upon the dark cross of your selfish desires, then, I say, you err in this unbelief and have not yet perceived, even far off, the Love of Christ.

You say that you have tasted of salvation in the Love of Christ. Are you saved from your temper, your irritability, your vanity, your personal dislikes, your judgement and condemnation of others? If not, from what are you saved, and wherein have you realized the transforming Love of Christ?

### *Divine Love is Selfless*

He who has realized the Love that is divine has become a new being, and has ceased to be swayed and dominated by the old elements of self. He is known for his patience, his purity, his self-control, his deep charity of heart, and his unalterable sweetness.

Divine or selfless Love is not a mere sentiment or emotion; it is a state of knowledge which destroys the dominion of evil and the belief in evil, and lifts the soul into the joyful realization of the supreme Good. To the divinely wise, knowledge and Love are one and inseparable.

It is toward the complete realization of this divine Love that the whole world is moving; it was for this purpose that the universe came into existence, and every grasping at happiness, every reaching out of the soul toward objects, ideas and ideals, is an effort to realize it. But the world does not realize this Love at present because it is grasping at the fleeting shadow and ignoring, in its blindness, the substance. And so suffering and sorrow continue, and must continue until the world, taught by its self-inflicted pains, discovers the Love that is selfless, the wisdom that is calm and full of peace.

And this Love, this Wisdom, this Peace, this

tranquil state of mind and heart may be attained to, may be realized by all who are willing and ready to yield up self, and who are prepared to humbly enter into a comprehension of all that giving up self involves.

## The Chains of Suffering

There is no arbitrary power in the universe, and the strongest chains of fate by which men are bound are self-forged. Men are chained to that which causes suffering because they desire to be so, because they love their chains, because they think their little dark prison of self is sweet and beautiful, and they are afraid that if they desert that prison they will lose all that is real and worth having.

> *Ye suffer from yourselves, none else compels,*
> *None other holds ye that ye live and die.*

And the indwelling power which forged the chains and built around itself the dark and narrow prison, can break away when it desires and wills to do so, and the soul does will to do so when it has discovered the worthlessness of its prison, when long suffering has prepared it for the reception of the boundless Light and Love.

As the shadow follows the form, and as smoke comes after the fire, so effect follows cause, and suffering and bliss follow the thoughts and deeds of men. There is no effect in the world around us but has its hidden or revealed cause, and that cause is in accordance with absolute justice. Men reap a harvest of suffering because in the near or distant past they have sown the seeds of evil; they reap a harvest of bliss also as a result of their own sowing of the seeds of good. Let a man meditate upon this, let him strive to understand it, and he will then begin to sow only seeds of good, and will burn up the tares and weeds which he has formerly grown in the garden of his heart.

### Understanding Selfless Love

The world does not understand the Love that is selfless because it is engrossed in the pursuit of its own pleasures, and cramped within the narrow limits of perishable interests, mistaking, in its ignorance, those pleasures and interests for real and abiding things. Caught in the flames of fleshly lusts, and burning with anguish, it sees not the pure and peaceful beauty of Truth. Feeding upon the swinish husks of error and self-delusion, it is shut out from the mansion of all-seeing Love.

Not having this Love, not understanding it, men institute innumerable reforms which involve no inward sacrifice, and each imagines that his reform is going to right the world forever, while he himself continues to propagate evil by engaging in it in his own heart. That only can be called reform which tends to reform the human heart, for all evil has its rise there, and not until the world, ceasing from selfishness and party strife, has learned the lesson of divine Love, will it realize the Golden Age of universal blessedness.

Let the rich cease to despise the poor, and the poor to condemn the rich; let the greedy learn how to give, and the lustful how to grow pure; let the partisan cease from strife, and the uncharitable begin to forgive; let the envious endeavor to rejoice with others, and the slanderers grow ashamed of their conduct. Let men and women take this course, and lo! the Golden Age is at hand. He, therefore, who purifies his own heart is the world's greatest benefactor.

Yet, though the world is, and will be for many ages to come, shut out from that Age of Gold, which is the realization of selfless Love, you, if you are willing, may enter it now, by rising above your selfish self; if you will pass from prejudice, hatred, and condemnation, to gentle and forgiving love.

Where hatred, dislike, and condemnation are, selfless Love does not abide. It resides only in the heart that has ceased all condemnation.

## Love Does Not Judge

You say, "How can I love the drunkard, the hypocrite, the sneak, the murderer? I am compelled to dislike and condemn such men." It is true you cannot love such men emotionally, but when you say that you must of necessity dislike and condemn them you will show that you are not acquainted with the Great overruling Love; for it is possible to attain to such a state of interior enlightenment as will enable you to perceive the train of causes by which these men have become as they are, to enter into their intense suffering, and to know the certainty of their ultimate purification. Possessed of such knowledge it will be utterly impossible for you any longer to dislike or condemn them, and you will always think of them with perfect calmness and deep compassion.

If you love people and speak of them with praise until they in some way thwart you, or do something of which you disapprove, and then you dislike them and speak of them with dispraise, you are not governed by the Love which is of God. If, in your heart, you are continually arraigning and condemning others, selfless Love is hidden from you.

He who knows that Love is at the heart of all things, and has realized the all-sufficing power of that Love, has no room in his heart for condemnation.

Men, not knowing this Love, constitute themselves judge and executioner of their fellows, forgetting that there is the Eternal Judge and Executioner, and insofar as men deviate from them in their own views, their particular reforms and methods, they brand them as fanatical, unbalanced, lacking judgement, sincerity, and honesty; insofar as others approximate to their own standard do they look upon them as being everything that is admirable.

Love does not so brand and classify men; does not seek to convert men to his own views, not to convince them of the superiority of his methods. Knowing the Law of Love, he lives it, and maintains the same calm attitude of mind and sweetness of heart towards all. The debased and the virtuous, the foolish and the wise, the learned and the unlearned, the selfish and the unselfish receive alike the benediction of his tranquil thought.

## *Attain Knowledge by Self-Discipline*

You can only attain to this supreme knowledge, this divine Love by unremitting endeavor in self-discipline, and by gaining victory after victory over yourself. Only the pure in heart see God, and when your heart is sufficiently purified you will enter into the New Birth, and the Love that does not die, nor change, nor end in pain and sorrow will be awakened within you, and you will be at peace.

He who strives for the attainment of divine Love is ever seeking to overcome the spirit of condemnation, for where there is pure spiritual knowledge, condemnation cannot exist, and only in the heart that has become incapable of condemnation is Love perfected and fully realized.

The Christian condemns the Atheist; the Atheist satirizes the Christian; the Catholic and Protestant are ceaselessly engaged in wordy warfare, and the spirit of strife and hatred rules where peace and love should be.

*He that hates his brother is a murderer*, a crucifier of the divine Spirit of Love; and until you can regard men of all religions and of no religion with the same impartial spirit, with all freedom from dislike, and with perfect equanimity, you have yet to strive for that Love which bestows upon its possessor freedom and salvation.

The realization of divine knowledge, selfless Love, utterly destroys the spirit of condemnation, disperses all evil, and lifts the consciousness to that height of pure vision where Love, Goodness, Justice are seen to be universal, supreme, all conquering, indestructible.

Train your mind in strong, impartial, and gentle thought; train your heart in purity and compassion; train your tongue to silence and to true and stainless speech; so shall you enter the way of holiness and peace, and shall ultimately realize the immortal Love. So living, without seeking to convert, you will convince; without arguing, you will teach; not cherishing ambition, the wise will find you out; and without striving to gain men's opinions, you will subdue their hearts. For Love is all-conquering, all-powerful; and the thoughts, and deeds, and words of Love can never perish.

To know that Love is universal, supreme, all-sufficing; to be freed from the trammels of evil; to be quit of the inward unrest; to know that all beings are striving to realize the Truth each in his or her own way; to be satisfied, sorrowless, serene; this is peace; this is gladness; this is immortality; this is Divinity; this is the realization of selfless Love.

## Entering into the Infinite

From the beginning of time, man, in spite of his bodily appetites and desires, in the midst of all his clinging to earthly and impermanent things, has ever been intuitively conscious of the limited, transient, and illusionary nature of his material existence, and in his sane and silent moments has tried to reach out into a comprehension of the Infinite, and has turned with tearful aspiration towards the restful Reality of the Eternal Heart.

While vainly imagining that the pleasures of earth are real and satisfying, pain and sorrow continually remind him of their unreal and unsatisfying nature. Ever striving to believe that complete satisfaction is to be found in material things, he is conscious of an inward and persistent revolt against this belief, which revolt is at once refutation of his essential mortality, and an inherent and imperishable proof that only in the immortal, the eternal, the infinite can he find abiding satisfaction and unbroken peace.

And here is the common ground of faith; here the root and spring of all religion; here the soul of Brotherhood and the heart of Love—that man is essentially and spiritually divine and eternal, and that, immersed in mortality and troubled with unrest, he is ever striving to enter into a consciousness of his real nature.

## *Man's Spirit is Infinite*

The spirit of humankind is inseparable from the Infinite, and can be satisfied with nothing short of the Infinite, and the burden of pain will continue to weigh upon each person's heart, and the shadows of sorrow to darken their pathway until, ceasing from wanderings in the dream world of matter, he or she comes back to their home in the reality of the Eternal.

As the smallest drop of water detached from the ocean contains all the qualities of the ocean, so each person, detached in consciousness from the Infinite, contains within themselves its likeness; and as the drop of water must, by the law of nature, ultimately find its way back to the ocean and lose itself in the silent depths, so must each person, by the unfailing law of our nature, at last return to our source, and lose ourself in the great ocean of the Infinite.

To become one with the Infinite is the goal of each man and woman. To enter into perfect harmony with the Eternal Law is Wisdom, Love and Peace. But this divine law is, and must ever be, incomprehensible to the merely personal. Personality, separateness, selfishness are one and the same, and the antithesis of wisdom and divinity. By the unqualified surrender of the personality, separateness and selfishness cease, and each enters into the possession of their divine heritage of immortality and infinity.

Such surrender of the personality is regarded by the worldly and selfish mind as the most grievous of all calamities, the most irreparable loss, yet it is the one supreme and incomparable blessing, the only real and lasting gain. The mind unenlightened upon the inner laws of being, and upon the nature and destiny of its own life, clings to transient appearances, things which have in them no enduring substantiality, and so clinging, perishes, for the time being, amid the shattered wreckage of its own illusions.

### The Body is Perishable

Men cling to and gratify the flesh as though it were going to last forever, and though they try to forget the nearness and inevitability of its dissolution, the dread of death and of the loss of all that they cling to clouds their happiest hours, and the chilling shadow of their own selfishness follows them like a remorseless ghost.

And with the accumulation of temporal comforts and luxuries, the divinity within man and woman alike is drugged, and they sink deeper and deeper into materiality, into the perishable life of the senses, and where there is sufficient intellect, theories concerning the immortality of the flesh come to be regarded as infallible truths.

When a person's soul is clouded with selfishness in any or every form, they lose the power of spiritual discrimination, and confuse the temporal with the eternal, the perishable with the permanent, mortality with immortality, and error with Truth. It is thus that the world has come to be filled with theories and speculations having no foundation in human experience. Every body of flesh contains within itself, from the hour of birth, the elements of its own destruction, and by the unalterable law of its own nature must it pass away.

The perishable in the universe can never become permanent; the permanent can never pass away; the mortal can never become immortal, the immortal can never die; the temporal cannot become eternal nor the eternal become temporal; appearance can never become reality, nor reality fade into appearance; error can never become Truth, nor can Truth become error. Man and women cannot immortalize the flesh, but, by becoming the flesh, by relinquishing all its inclinations, they can enter the region of immortality. "God alone hath immortality," and only by realizing the God state of consciousness do men and women enter into immortality.

## *Practice Self-Denial*

All nature in its myriad forms of life is changeable, impermanent, unenduring. Only the informing Principle of nature endures. Nature is many, and is marked by separation. The informing Principle is One, and is marked by unity. By overcoming the senses and the selfishness within, which is the overcoming of nature, man emerges from the hard shell of the personal and illusionary, and wings himself into the glorious light of the impersonal, the region of universal Truth, out of which all perishable forms come.

Let men, therefore, practice self-denial; let them conquer their animal inclinations; let them refuse to be enslaved by luxury and pleasure; let them practice virtue, and grow daily into higher and ever higher virtue, until at last they grow into the Divine, and enter into both the practice and comprehension of humility, meekness, forgiveness, compassion and love, which practice and comprehension constitute Divinity.

"Goodwill gives insight," and only he who has so conquered his personality that he has but one attitude of mind, that of goodwill toward all creatures, is possessed of divine insight, and is capable of distinguishing the true from the false. The supremely good man is therefore the wise man, the divine man, the enlightened seer, the knower of the Eternal.

Where you find unbroken gentleness, enduring patience, sublime lowliness, graciousness of speech, self-control, self-forgetfulness, and deep and abounding sympathy, look there for the highest wisdom, seek the company of such a one, for he has realized the Divine, he lives with the Eternal, he has become one with the Infinite. Believe not him that is impatient, given to anger, boastful, who clings to pleasure and refuses to renounce his selfish gratifications, and who practices not goodwill and far-reaching compassion, for such a one hath not wisdom, vain is all his knowledge, and his works and words will perish, for they are grounded on that which passes away.

Let a man abandon self, let him overcome the world, let him deny the personal; by this pathway only can he enter into the heart of the Infinite.

The world, the body, the personality are mirages upon the desert of time; transitory dreams in the dark night of spiritual slumber, and those who have crossed the desert, those who are spiritually awakened, have alone comprehended the Universal Reality where all appearances are dispersed and dreaming and delusion are destroyed.

### Entering into the Infinite

There is one Great Law which exacts unconditional obedience, one unifying principle which is the basis of all diversity, one eternal Truth wherein all the problems of earth pass away like shadows. To realize this Law, this Truth, is to enter into the Infinite, is to become one with the Eternal.

To center one's life in the Great Law of Love is to enter into rest, harmony and peace. To refrain from all participation in evil and discord; to cease from all resistance to evil, and from the omission of that which is good, and to fall back upon unswerving obedience to the holy calm within, is to enter into the inmost heart of things, is to attain to a living, conscious experience of that eternal and infinite principle which must ever remain a hidden mystery to the merely perceptive intellect. Until this principle is realized, the soul is not established in peace, and he who so realizes is truly wise; not wise with the wisdom of the learned, but with the simplicity of a blameless heart and of divine humanhood.

To enter into a realization of the Infinite and Eternal is to rise superior to time, and the world, and the body, which comprise the kingdom of darkness; and is to become established in immortality, Heaven, and the Spirit, which make up the Empire of Light.

Entering into the Infinite is not a mere theory or sentiment. It is a vital experience which is the result of the assiduous practice in inward purification. When the body is no longer believed to be, even remotely, the real man; when all appetites and desires are thoroughly subdued and purified; when the emotions are rested and calm, and when the oscillation of the intellect ceases and perfect poise is secured, then, and not till then, does consciousness become one with the Infinite; not until then is childlike wisdom and profound peace secured.

## Love of Self Shuts Out Truth

Men grow weary and gray over the dark problems of life, and finally pass away and leave them unsolved because they cannot see their way out of the darkness of the personality, being too much engrossed in its limitations. Seeking to save his personal life, man forfeits the greater impersonal Life in Truth; clinging to the perishable, he is shut out from a knowledge of the Eternal.

By the surrender of self all difficulties are overcome, and there is no error in the universe but the fire of inward sacrifice will burn it up like chaff; no problem, however great, but will disappear like a shadow under the searching light of self-denial. Problems exist only in our self-created illusions, and they vanish away when self is yielded up. Self and error are synonymous. Error is involved in the darkness of unfathomable complexity, but eternal simplicity is the glory of Truth.

Love of self shuts men out from the Truth, and seeking their own personal happiness they lose the deeper, purer, and more abiding bliss.

Says Carlyle—"There is in man a higher than love of happiness. He can do without happiness, and instead thereof find blessedness...Love not pleasure, love God. This is the Everlasting Yea, wherein all contradiction is solved; wherein whoso walks and works, it is well with him."

He who has yielded up that self, that personality that men most love, and to which they cling with such fierce tenacity, has left behind him all perplexity, and has entered into a simplicity so profoundly simple as to be looked upon by the world, involved as it is in a network of error, as foolishness. Yet such a one has realized the highest wisdom, and is at rest in the infinite. He "accomplishes without striving," and all problems melt before him, for he has entered the region of reality, and deals, not with changing effects, but with the unchanging principles of things.

He is enlightened with a wisdom which is as superior to the process of reasoning, as reason is to animality. Having yielded up his lusts, his errors, his opinions and prejudices, he has entered into possession of the knowledge of God, having slain the selfish desire for heaven, and along with it the ignorant fear of hell; having relinquished even the love of life itself, he has gained supreme bliss and Life Eternal, the Life which bridges life and death, and knows its own immortality. Having yielded up all without reservation, he has gained all, and rests in peace on the bosom of the Infinite.

## Trust in the Supreme Good

Only he who has become so free from self as to be equally content to be annihilated as to live, or to live as to be annihilated, is fit to enter into the Infinite. Only he who, ceasing to trust his perishable self, has learned to trust in boundless measure the Great Law, the Supreme Good, is prepared to partake of undying bliss.

For such a one there is no more regret, nor disappointment, nor remorse, for where all selfishness has ceased these sufferings cannot be; and whatever happens to him he knows that it is for his own good, and he is content, being no longer the servant of the self, but the servant of the Supreme. He is no longer affected by the changes of earth, and when he hears of wars and rumors of wars his peace is not disturbed, and where men grow angry and cynical and quarrelsome, he bestows compassion and love. Though appearances may contradict it, he knows that the world is progressing and that:

> *Through its laughing and its weeping,*
> *Through its living and its keeping,*
> *Through its follies and its labors, weaving in*
> *and out of sight,*

*To the end from the beginning,*
*Through all virtue and all sinning,*
*Reeled from God's great spool of Progress, runs*
*the golden thread of light.*

When a fierce storm is raging none are angered about it, because they know it will quickly pass away, and when the storms of contention are devastating the world, the wise man, looking with the eye of Truth and pity, knows that it will pass away, and that out of the wreckage of broken hearts which it leaves behind, the immortal Temple of Wisdom will be built.

Sublimely patient; infinitely compassionate; deep, silent, and pure, his very presence is a benediction; and when he speaks men ponder his words in their hearts, and by them rise to higher levels of attainment. Such is he who has entered into the Infinite, who by the power of utmost sacrifice has solved that sacred mystery of life.

# Saints, Sages, & Saviors: The Law of Service

THE SPIRIT OF LOVE which is manifested as a perfect and rounded life, is the crown of being and the supreme end of knowledge upon this earth. The measure of a man's truth is the measure of his love, and Truth is far removed from him whose life is not governed by Love. The intolerant and condemnatory, even though they profess the highest religion, have the smallest measure of Truth; while those who exercise patience, and who listen calmly and dispassionately to all sides, and both arrive themselves at, and incline others to, thoughtful and unbiased conclusions upon all problems and issues, have Truth in fullest measure.

The final test of wisdom is this—how does a man live? What spirit does he manifest? How does he act under trial and temptation? Many men boast of being in possession of Truth who are continually swayed by grief, disappointment, and passion, and who sink under the first little trial that comes along. Truth is nothing if not unchangeable, and insofar as a man takes his stand upon Truth does he become steadfast in virtue, does he rise superior to his passions and emotions and changeable personality.

Men formulate perishable dogmas, and call them Truth. Truth cannot be formulated; it is ineffable, and ever beyond the reach of intellect. It can only be experienced by practice: it can only be manifested as a stainless heart and a perfect life.

Who, then, in the midst of the ceaseless pandemonium of schools and creeds and parties, has the Truth? He who lives it. He who practices it. He who, having risen above that pandemonium by overcoming himself, no longer engages in it, but sits apart, quiet, subdued, calm, and self-possessed, freed from all strife, all bias, all condemnation, and bestows upon all the glad and unselfish love of the divinity within him.

## Words Cannot Prove Truth

He who is patient, calm, gentle, and forgiving under all circumstances, manifests the Truth. Truth will never be proved by wordy arguments and learned treatises, for if men do not perceive Truth in infinite patience, undying forgiveness, and all embracing compassion, no words can ever prove it to them.

It is an easy matter for the passionate to be calm and patient when they are alone, or are in the midst of calmness. It is equally easy for the uncharitable to be gentle and kind when they are dealt kindly with, but he who retains his patience and calmness under all trial, who remains sublimely meek and gentle under the most trying circumstances, he, and he alone, is possessed of the spotless Truth.

And this is so because such lofty virtues belong to the Divine, and can only be manifested by one who has attained to the highest wisdom, who has relinquished his passionate and self-seeking nature, who has realized the supreme and unchangeable Law, and has brought himself into harmony with it.

Let men, therefore, cease from vain and passionate arguments about Truth, and let them think and say and do those things which make for harmony, peace, love and goodwill. Let them practice heart-virtue, and search humbly and diligently for the Truth which frees the soul from all error and sin, from all that blights the human heart, and that darkens, as with unending night, the pathway of the wandering souls of earth.

## *The Law of Love*

There is one great all-embracing Law which is the foundation and cause of the universe, the Law of Love. It has been called by many names in various countries and at various times, but behind all its names the same unalterable Law may be discovered by the eye of Truth. Names, religions, personalities pass away, but the Law of Love remains. To become possessed of the knowledge of this Law, to enter into conscious harmony with it, is to become immortal, invincible, indestructible.

It is because of the effort of the soul to realize this Law that men and women come again and again to live, to suffer, and to die; and when realized suffering ceases, personality is dispersed, and the fleshly life and death are destroyed, for consciousness becomes one with the Eternal.

The Law is absolutely impersonal, and its highest manifested expression is that of Service. When the purified heart has realized Truth, it is called upon to make the last, the greatest and holiest sacrifice, the sacrifice of the well-earned enjoyment of Truth. It is by virtue of this sacrifice that the divinely emancipated soul comes to dwell among men and women, clothed with a body of flesh, content to dwell among the lowliest and least, and to be esteemed the servant of all humankind.

### Humility is the Mark of Greatness

That sublime humility which is manifested by the world's saviors is the seal of Godhead, and he who has annihilated the personality, and has become a living, visible manifestation of the impersonal, eternal, boundless Spirit of Love, is alone singled out as worthy to receive the unstinted worship of posterity. He only who succeeds in humbling himself with that divine humility which is not only the extinction of self, but is also the pouring out upon all the spirit of unselfish love, is exalted above measure, and given spiritual dominion in the hearts of humankind.

All the great spiritual teachers have denied themselves personal luxuries, comforts, and rewards, have renounced temporal power, and have lived and taught the limitless and impersonal Truth. Compare their lives and teachings, and you will find the same simplicity, the same self-sacrifice, the same humility, love, and peace both lived and preached by them. They taught the same eternal Principles, the realization of which destroys all evil.

Those who have been hailed and worshipped as

the saviors of mankind are manifestations of the Great impersonal Law, and being such, were free from passion and prejudice, and having no opinions, and no special letter of doctrine to preach and defend, they never sought to convert or proselytize. Living in the highest Goodness, the supreme Perfection, their sole object was to uplift mankind by manifesting that Goodness in thought, word, and deed. They stand between man the personal and God the impersonal, and serve as exemplary types for the salvation of self-enslaved mankind.

Men who are immersed in self, and who cannot comprehend the Goodness that is absolutely impersonal, deny divinity to all saviors except their own, and thus introduce personal hatred and doctrinal controversy, and, while defending their own particular views with passion, look upon each other as being heathens or infidels, and so render null and void, as far as their lives are concerned, the unselfish beauty and holy grandeur of the lives and teachings of their own Masters. Truth cannot be limited; it can never be the special prerogative of any man, school, or nation, and when personality steps in, truth is lost.

The glory alike of the saint, the sage, and the savior is this—that he has realized the most profound lowliness, the most sublime unselfishness; having given up all, even his own personality, all his works are holy and enduring, for they are freed from every taint of self. He gives, yet never thinks of receiving; he works without regretting the past or anticipating the future, and never looks for reward.

## Sowing the Seeds

When the farmer has tilled and dressed his land and put in the seed, he knows that he has done all that he can possibly do, and that now he must trust to the elements, and wait patiently for the course of time to bring about the harvest, and that no amount of expectancy on his part will affect the result. Even so, he who has realized truth goes forth as a sower of seeds of goodness, purity, love and peace, without expectancy, and never looking for results, knowing that there is the Great Overruling Law which brings about its own harvest in due time, and which is alike the source of preservation and destruction.

Men, not understanding the divine simplicity of a profoundly unselfish heart, look upon their particular savior as the manifestation of a special miracle, as being something entirely apart and distinct from the nature of things, and as being, in his ethical excellence, eternally unapproachable by the whole of mankind. This attitude of unbelief (for such it is) in the divine perfectibility of man, paralyzes effort, and binds the souls of men as with strong ropes to sin and suffering.

Jesus "grew in wisdom" and was "perfected by suffering." What Jesus was, he became such; what Buddha was, he became such; and every holy man became such by unremitting perseverance in self-sacrifice. Once this is recognized, one realizes that by watchful effort and hopeful perseverance you can rise above your lower nature, and great and glorious will be the prospects of attainment that will open out before you. Buddha vowed that he would not relax his efforts until he arrived at the state of perfection, and he accomplished his purpose.

What the saints, sages and saviors have accomplished, you likewise may accomplish if you will only tread the way which they trod and pointed out, the way of self-sacrifice, or self-denying service.

Truth is very simple. It says, "Give up self. Come unto me [away from all that defiles] and I will give you rest." All the mountains of commentary that have been piled upon it cannot hide it from the heart that is earnestly seeking for righteousness. It does not require learning; it can be known in spite of learning. Disguised under many forms by erring, self-seeking man, the beautiful simplicity and clear transparency of Truth remains unaltered and undimmed, and the selfish heart enters into and partakes of its shining radiance. Not by weaving complex theories, not by building up speculative philosophies is Truth realized; but by weaving the web of inward purity, by building up the Temple of a stainless life is Truth realized.

## The Curbing of Passions

He who enters upon this holy way begins by restraining his passions. This is virtue, and is the beginning of sainthood, and sainthood is the beginning of holiness. The entirely worldly man gratifies all his desires, and practices no more restraint than the law of the land in which he lives demands; the virtuous man restrains his passions; the saint attacks the enemy of Truth in its stronghold within his own heart, and restrains all selfish and impure thoughts; while the holy man is he who is free from passion and all impure thought, and to whom goodness and purity have become as natural as scent and color are to the flower. The holy man is divinely wise; he alone knows Truth in its fullness, and has entered into abiding rest and peace. For him evil has ceased; it has disappeared in the universal light of the All-Good. Holiness is the badge of wisdom.

> *Said Krishna to the Prince Arjuna—*
> *Humbleness, truthfulness, and harmlessness,*
> *Patience and honor, reverence for the wise,*
> *Purity, constancy, control of self,*
> *Contempt of sense-delights, self-sacrifice,*
> *Perception of the certitude of ill*
> *In birth, death, age, disease, suffering and sin;*
> *An ever tranquil heart in fortunes good*
> *And fortunes evil,...*
> *...Endeavors resolute*
> *To reach perception of the utmost soul,*
> *And grace to understand what gain it were*
> *So to attain—this is true wisdom, Prince!*
> *And what is otherwise is ignorance!*

### True Service is Forgetting Self

Whoever fights ceaselessly against his own self-ishness, and strives to supplant it with all-embracing love is a saint, whether he live in a cottage or in the midst of riches and influence; or whether he preaches or remains obscure.

To the worldling, who is beginning to aspire toward higher things, the saint, such as a sweet St. Francis of Assisi, or a conquering St. Anthony, is a glorious and inspiring spectacle; to the saint, an equally enrapturing sight is that of the sage, sitting serene and holy, the conqueror of sin and sorrow, no more tormented by regret and remorse, and whom even temptation can never reach; and yet even the sage is drawn on by a still more glorious vision, that of the savior actively manifesting his knowledge in selfless works, and rendering his divinity more potent for good by sinking himself in the throbbing, sorrowing, aspiring heart of humankind.

And this only is true service—to forget oneself in love towards all, to lose oneself in working for the whole. O you vain and foolish man, who thinks many words can save; who, chained to error, talks loudly about himself, his work, and his many sacrifices, and magnifies his own importance; know this, that though your fame fill the whole earth, all your work shall come to dust, and be reckoned lower than the least in the Kingdom of Truth!

Only the work that is impersonal can live; the works of self are both powerless and perishable.

Where duties, however humble, are done without self interest, and with joyful sacrifice, there is true service and enduring work. Where deeds, however brilliant and apparently successful, are done from love of self, there is ignorance of the Law of Service, and the work perishes.

It is given to the world to learn one great and divine lesson, the lesson of absolute unselfishness. The saints, sages, and saviors of all time are they who have submitted themselves to this task, and have learned and lived it. All the Scriptures of the world are framed to teach this one lesson; all the great teachers reiterate it. It is too simple for the world which, scorning it, stumbles along in the complex ways of selfishness.

A pure heart is the end of all religion and the beginning of divinity. To search for this Righteousness is to walk the Way of Truth and Peace, and he or she who enters this Way will soon perceive that Immortality which is independent of birth and death, and will realize that in the Divine economy of the universe the humblest effort is not lost.

The divinity of Krishna, a Gautama, or a Jesus is the crowning glory of self-denial, the end of the soul's pilgrimage in matter and mortality, and the world will not have finished its long journey until every soul has become as these, and has entered into blissful realization of its own divinity.

# The Realization
of Perfect Peace

IN THE EXTERNAL UNIVERSE there is ceaseless turmoil, change and unrest; at the heart of all things there is undisturbed repose; in this silence dwelleth the Eternal.

Man partakes of this duality, and both the surface change and disquietude, and the deep-seated eternal abode of Peace are contained within him.

As there are silent depths in the ocean which the fiercest storm cannot reach, so there are silent, holy depths in the heart of man which the storms of sin and sorrow can never disturb. To reach this silence and to live consciously in it is peace.

Discord is plentiful in the outward world, but unbroken harmony holds sway at the heart of the universe. The human soul, torn by discordant passion and grief, reaches blindly toward the harmony of the sinless state, and to reach this state and to live consciously in it is peace.

Hatred severs human lives, fosters persecution, and hurls nations into ruthless war, yet men and women, though they do not understand why, retain some measure of faith in the overshadowing of a Perfect Love; and to reach this love and to live consciously in it is peace.

And this inward peace, this silence, this harmony, this Love, is the Kingdom of Heaven, which is so difficult to reach because few are willing to give up themselves and to become as little children.

*Heaven's gate is very narrow and minute,*
*It cannot be perceived by foolish men*
*Blinded by vain illusions of the world;*
*Even the clear-sighted who discern the way,*
*And seek to enter, find the portal barred,*
*And hard to be unlocked. Its massive bolts*
*Are pride and passion, avarice and lust.*

Men cry peace! peace! where there is no peace, but on the contrary, discord, and disquietude and strife. Apart from that Wisdom which is inseparable from self-renunciation, there can be no real and abiding peace.

### Self-Control Leads to Peace

The peace which results from social comfort, passing gratification, or worldly victory is brief in its nature, and is burnt up in the heat of fiery trial. Only the Peace of Heaven endures through all trial, and only the selfless heart can know the Peace of Heaven.

Holiness alone is undying peace. Self-control leads to it, and the ever-increasing Light of Wisdom guides the pilgrim on his way. It is partaken of in a measure as soon as the path of virtue is entered upon, but it is only realized in its fullness when self disappears in the consummation of a stainless life.

> *This is peace*
> *To conquer love of self and lust of life,*
> *To tear deep-rooted passion from the heart*
> *To still the inward strife.*

If, O reader! you would realize the Light that never fades, the joy that never ends, and the tranquility that cannot be disturbed; if you would leave behind your sins, your sorrow, your anxieties and perplexities; if, I say, you would partake of this salvation, this supremely glorious Life, then conquer yourself. Bring every thought, every impulse, every desire into perfect obedience to the divine power resident within you. There is no other way to peace but this, and if you refuse to walk it, your much praying and your strict adherence to ritual will be fruitless and unavailing, and neither gods nor angels can help you. Only to him that overcometh is given the white stone of the regenerate life, on which is written the New and Ineffable Name.

Come away, for a while, from external things, from the pleasures of the senses, from the arguments of the intellect, from the noise and excitements of the world, and withdraw yourself into the innermost chamber of your heart, and there, free from the sacrilegious intrusion of all selfish desires, you will find deep silence, a holy calm, a blissful repose, and you will rest awhile in that holy place, and will meditate there, the faultless eye of Truth will open within you, and you will see things as they really are.

This holy place within you is your real and eternal self; it is the divine within you; and only when you identify yourself with it can you be said to be "clothed and in your right mind." It is the abode of peace, the temple of wisdom, the dwelling-place of immortality. Apart from this inward resting-place, this Mount of Vision, there can be no true peace, no knowledge of the Divine, and if you can remain there for one minute, one hour, or one day, it is possible for you to remain there always.

## *You Must Walk the Way Yourself*

All your sins and sorrows, your fears and anxieties are your own, and you can cling to them or you can give them up. Of your own accord you cling to your unrest; of your own accord you can come to abiding peace. No one else can give up sin for you; you must give it up yourself. The greatest teacher can do no more than walk the way of truth for himself, and point it out to you; you yourself must walk it for yourself. You can obtain freedom and peace alone by your own efforts, by yielding up that which binds the soul, and which is destructive of peace.

The angels of divine peace and joy are always at hand, and if you do not see them, and hear them, and dwell with them, it is because you shut yourself out from them, and prefer the company of the spirits of evil within you. You are what you will to be, what you wish to be, what you prefer to be. You can commence to purify yourself, and by so doing can arrive at peace, or you can refuse to purify yourself, and so remain with suffering.

Step aside, then; come out of the fret and fever of

life; away from the scorching heat of self, and enter the inward resting-place where the cooling airs of peace will calm, renew, and restore you.

Come out of the storms of sin and anguish. Why be troubled and tempest-tossed when the haven of peace is so near?

Give up all self-seeking; give up self, and lo! the Peace of God is yours!

Subdue the animal within you; conquer every selfish uprising, every discordant voice; transmute the base metals of your selfish nature into the unalloyed gold of Love, and you shall realize the Life of Perfect Peace. Thus subduing, thus conquering, thus transmuting, you will, O reader! while living in the flesh, cross the dark waters of mortality, and will reach that Shore upon which the storms of sorrow never beat, and where sin and suffering and dark uncertainty cannot come. Standing upon that Shore, holy, compassionate, awakened, and self-possessed and glad with unending gladness, you will realize that,

> *Never the Spirit was born, the Spirit will*
>     *cease to be never;*
> *Never was time it was not, end and beginning*
>     *are dreams;*

*the Spirit forever;*
*Death hath not touched it at all.*

You will then know the meaning of Sin, of Sorrow, of Suffering, and that the end thereof is Wisdom; will know the cause and the effect of existence.

And with this realization you will enter into rest, for this is the bliss of immortality, this is the unchangeable gladness, this the untrammeled knowledge, undefiled Wisdom, and undying Love; this, and this only, is the realization of Perfect Peace.

# Book Five

# Entering the Kingdom

# TABLE OF CONTENTS

# The Soul's Great Need

*I sought the world, but Peace was not there;*
*I courted learning, but Truth was not revealed;*
*I sojourned with philosophy, but my heart was*
*sore with vanity.*
*And I cried, Where is Peace to be found!*
*And where is the hiding place of truth!*
*—Filius Lucis*

EVERY HUMAN SOUL IS IN NEED. The expression of that need varies with individuals, but there is not one soul that does not feel it in some degree. It is a spiritual and casual need which takes the form, in souls of a particular development, of a deep and inexpressible hunger which the outward things of life, however abundantly they may be possessed, can never satisfy. Yet the majority, imperfect in knowledge and misled by appearances, seek to satisfy this hunger by striving for material possessions, believing that these will satisfy their need, and bring them peace.

Every soul, consciously or unconsciously, hungers for righteousness, and every soul seeks to gratify that hunger in its own particular way, and in accordance with its own particular state of knowledge. The hunger is one, and the righteousness is one, but the pathways by which righteousness is sought are many.

They who seek consciously are blessed, and shall shortly find that final and permanent satisfaction of soul which righteousness alone can give, for they have come into a knowledge of the true path.

They who seek unconsciously, although for a time they may bathe in a sea of pleasure, are not blessed, for they are carving out for themselves pathways of suffering over which they must walk with torn and wounded feet, and their hunger will increase, and the soul will cry out for its lost heritage—the eternal heritage of righteousness.

Not in any of the three worlds [waking, dream and sleep] can the soul find lasting satisfaction, apart from the realization of righteousness. Bodied or disembodied, it is ceaselessly driven on by the discipline of suffering, until at last, in its extremity, it flies to its only refuge—the refuge of righteousness—and finds that joy, satisfaction, and peace which it had so long and so vainly sought.

## The Principle of Righteousness

The great need of the soul, then, is the need of this permanent principle, called righteousness, on which it may stand securely and restfully amid the tempest of earthly existence, no more bewildered, and whereon it may build the mansion of a beautiful, peaceful, and perfect life.

It is the realization of this principle where the Kingdom of Heaven, the abiding home of the soul, resides, and which is the source and storehouse of every permanent blessing. Finding it, all is found; not finding it, all is lost. It is an attitude of mind, a state of consciousness, an ineffable knowledge, in which the struggle for existence ceases, and the soul finds itself at rest in the midst of plenty, where its great need, yea, its every need, is satisfied, without strife and without fear. Blessed are they who earnestly and intelligently seek, for it is impossible that such should seek in vain.

# The Competitive Laws
# & the Law of Love

*When I am pure*
*I shall have solved the mystery of life,*
*I am sure*
*(When I am free from hatred, lust and strife)*
*I am in truth, and Truth abides in me.*
*I shall be safe and sane and wholly free*
*When I am pure.*

IT HAS BEEN SAID THAT the laws of Nature are cruel; it has likewise been said that they are kind. The one statement is the result of dwelling exclusively upon the fiercely competitive aspect of Nature; the other results from viewing only the protective and kindly aspect. In reality, natural laws are neither cruel or kind; they are absolutely just—are, in fact, the outworking of the indestructible principle of justice itself.

The cruelty, and consequent suffering, which is so prevalent in Nature, is not inherent in the heart and substance of life; it is a passing phase of evolution, a painful experience, which will ultimately ripen into the fruit of a more perfect knowledge; a dark night of ignorance and unrest, leading to a glorious morning of joy and peace.

When a helpless child is burnt to death, we do not ascribe cruelty to the working of the natural law by virtue of which the child was consumed; we infer ignorance in the child, or carelessness on the part of its guardians. Even so, men and creatures are daily being consumed in the invisible flames of passion, succumbing to the ceaseless interplay of those fiery psychic forces which, in their ignorance, they do not understand, but which they shall at last learn how to control and use to their own protection, and not, as at present, foolishly employ them to their own destruction.

To understand, control and harmoniously adjust the invisible forces of its own soul is the ultimate destiny of every being and creature. Some men and women, in the past, have accomplished this supreme and exalted purpose; some, in the present, have likewise succeeded, and, until this is done, that place of rest wherein one receives all that is necessary for one's well-being and happiness, without striving, and with freedom from pain, cannot be entered.

## Understanding Competition

In an age like the present, when, in all civilized countries, the string of life is strained to its highest pitch, when men and women, striving each with each in every department of life for the vanities and material possessions of this perishable existence, have developed competition to the utmost limit of endurance—in such an age the sublimest heights of knowledge are scaled, the supremest spiritual conquests are achieved; for when the soul is most tired, its need is greatest, and where the need is great, great will be the effort. Where, also, the temptations are powerful, the greater and more enduring will be the victory.

Men love the competitive strife with their fellows, while it promises, and seems to bring them gain and happiness; but when the inevitable reaction comes, and the cold steel of selfish strife which their own hands have forged enters their own hearts, then, and not till then, do they seek a better way.

"Blessed are they that mourn,"—that have come

to the end of strife, and have found the pain and sorrow to which it leads; for unto them, and unto them only, can open the door which leads to the Kingdom of Peace.

In searching for this Kingdom, it is necessary to fully understand the nature of that which prevents its realization—namely, the strife of nature, the competitive laws operative in human affairs, and the universal unrest, insecurity and fear which accompany these factors; for without such an understanding there can be no sound comprehension as to what constitutes the true and false in life, and therefore no real spiritual advancement.

Before the true can be apprehended and enjoyed, the false must be unveiled; before the real can be perceived as the real, the illusions which distort it must be dispersed; and before the limitless expanse of Truth can open before us, the limited experience which is confined to the world of visible and superficial effects must be transcended.

Let, therefore, those of my readers who are thoughtful and earnest, and who are diligently seeking, or are willing to seek, for that basis of thought and conduct which shall simplify and harmonize the bewildering complexities and inequalities of life, walk with me step by step as I open up the way to the Kingdom; first descending into Hell (the world of strife and self-seeking) in order that, having comprehended its intricate ways, we may afterwards ascend into Heaven (the world of Peace and Love).

## *The Selfishness of Competition*

It is the custom in my household, during the hard frosts of winter, to put out food for the birds, and it is a noticeable fact that these creatures, when they are really starving, live together most amicably, huddling together to keep each other warm, and refraining from all strife; and if a small quantity of food be given them they will eat it with comparative freedom from contention; but let a quantity of food which is more than sufficient for all be thrown to them, and fighting over the coveted supply at once ensues.

Occasionally we would put out a whole loaf of bread, and then the contention of the birds became fierce and prolonged, although there was more than they could possibly eat during several days. Some, having gorged themselves until they could eat no more, would stand upon the loaf and hover round it, pecking fiercely at all newcomers, and endeavoring to prevent them from obtaining any of the food. And along with this fierce contention there was noticeably a great fear. With each mouthful of food taken, the birds would look around in nervous terror, apprehensive of losing their food or their lives.

### *Abundance Causes Selfishness*

In this simple incident we have an illustration—crude, perhaps, but true—of the basis and outworking of the competitive laws in Nature and in human affairs. It is not scarcity that produces competition, *it is abundance*; so that the richer and more luxurious a nation becomes, the keener and fiercer becomes the competition for securing the necessaries and luxuries of life.

Let famine overtake a nation, and at once compassion and sympathy take the place of competitive strife; and, in the blessedness of giving and receiving, men enjoy a foretaste of that heavenly bliss which the spiritually wise have found, and which all shall ultimately reach.

The fact that abundance, and not scarcity, creates competition, should be held constantly in mind by the reader during the perusal of this book, as it throws a searching light not only on the statements herein contained, but upon every problem relating to social life and human conduct. Moreover, if it be deeply and earnestly meditated upon, and its lessons applied to individual conduct, it will make plain the Way which leads to the Kingdom.

Let us now search out the *cause* of this fact, in order that the evils connected with it may be transcended.

### Competition Causes Suffering

Every phenomenon in social and national life (as in Nature) is an effect, and all these effects are embodied by a cause which is not remote and detached, but which is the immediate soul and life of the effect itself. As the seed is contained in the flower, and the flower in the seed, so the relation of cause and effect is intimate and inseparable. An effect also is vivified and propagated, not by any life inherent in itself, but by the life and impulse existing in the cause.

Looking out upon the world, we behold it as an arena of strife in which individuals, communities, and nations are constantly engaged in struggle, striving with each other for superiority, and for the largest share of worldly possessions.

We see, also, that the weaker fall out defeated, and that the strong—those who are equipped to pursue the combat with undiminished ardor—obtain the victory, and enter into possession. And along with this struggle we see the suffering which is inevitably connected with it—men and women, broken down with the weight of their responsibilities, failing in their efforts and losing all; families and communities broken up, and nations subdued and subordinated.

We see seas of tears, telling of unspeakable anguish and grief; we see painful partings and early and unnatural deaths; and we know that this life of strife, when stripped of its surface appearances, is largely a life of sorrow.

Such, briefly sketched, are the phenomena connected with that aspect of human life with which we are now dealing; such are the effects as we see them; and they have one common cause which is found in the human heart itself.

### Inner and Outer Activities

As all the multiform varieties of plant life have one common soil from which to draw their sustenance, and by virtue of which they live and thrive, so all the varied activities of human life are rooted in, and draw their vitality from, one common source— *the human heart*. The cause of all suffering and of all happiness resides, not in the outer activities of human life, but in the inner activities of the heart and mind; and every external agency is sustained by the life which it derives from human conduct.

The organized life-principle in man carves for itself outward channels along which it can pour its pent-up energies, makes for itself vehicles through which it can manifest its potency and reap its experience, and, as a result, we have our religious, social and political organizations.

All the visible manifestations of human life, then, are effects; and as such, although they may possess a reflex action, they can never be causes, but must remain forever what they are—*dead effects*, galvanized into life by an enduring and profound cause.

### Selfishness, the Root of Competition

It is the custom of men to wander about in this world of effects, and to mistake its illusions for realities, eternally transposing and readjusting these effects in order to arrive at a solution of human problems, instead of reaching down to the underlying cause which is at once the center of unification and the basis upon which to build a peace-giving solution of human life.

The strife of the world in all its forms, whether it be war, social or political quarreling, sectarian hatred, private disputes or commercial competition, has its origin in one common cause, namely, *individual selfishness*. And I employ this term selfishness in a far-reaching sense; in it I include all forms of self-love and egotism—I mean by it the desire to pander to, and preserve at all costs, the personality.

This element of selfishness is the life and soul of competition, and of the competitive laws. Apart from it they have no existence. But in the life of every individual in whose heart selfishness in any form is harbored, these laws are brought into play, and the individual is subject to them.

Innumerable economic systems have failed, and must fail, to exterminate the strife of the world. They are the outcome of the delusion that outward systems of government are the causes of that strife, whereas they are but the visible and transient effect of the *inward strife*, the channels through which it must necessarily manifest itself. To destroy the channel is, and must ever be ineffectual, as the inward energy will immediately make for itself another, and still another and another.

Strife cannot cease; and the competitive laws

*must prevail so long as selfishness is fostered in the heart.* All reforms fail where this element is ignored or unaccounted for; all reforms will succeed where it is recognized, and steps are taken for its removal.

## Selfishness Must Be Uprooted

Selfishness, then, is the root cause of competition, the foundation on which all competitive systems rest, and the sustaining source of the competitive laws. It will thus be seen that all competitive systems, all the visible activities of the struggle of man with man, are as the leaves and branches of a tree which overspreads the whole earth, the root of that tree being *individual selfishness*, and the ripened fruits of which are pain and sorrow.

This tree cannot be destroyed by merely lopping off its branches; to do this effectively, *the root must be destroyed.* To introduce measures in the form of changed external conditions is merely lopping off the branches; and as the cutting away of certain branches of a tree gives added vigor to those which remain, even so the very means which are taken to curtail the competitive strife, when those means deal entirely with its outward effects, will but add strength and vigor to the tree whose roots are all the time being fostered and encouraged in the human heart. The most that even legislation can do is to prune the branches, and so prevent the tree from altogether running wild.

### The "Garden City" is Unselfish Love

Great efforts are now being put forward to found a "Garden City," which shall be a veritable Eden planted in the midst of orchards, and whose inhabitants shall live in comfort and comparative repose. And beautiful and laudable are all such efforts when they are prompted by unselfish love. But such a city cannot exist, or cannot long remain the Eden which it aims to be in its outward form, unless the majority of its inhabitants have subdued and conquered the inward selfishness.

Even one form of selfishness, namely, *self-indulgence*, if fostered by its inhabitants, will completely undermine that city, leveling its orchards to the ground, converting many of its beautiful dwellings into competitive marts, and obnoxious centers for the personal gratification of appetite, and some of its buildings into institutions for the maintenance of order; and upon its public spaces will rise jails, asylums, and orphanages, for where the spirit of self-indulgence is, the means for its gratification will be immediately adopted, without considering the good of others or of the community (for selfishness is always blind), and the fruits of that gratification will be rapidly reaped.

The building of pleasant houses and the planting of beautiful gardens can never, of itself, constitute a Garden City unless its inhabitants have learned that self-sacrifice is better than self-protection, and have first established in their own hearts the Garden City of unselfish love. And when a sufficient number of men and women have done this, the Garden City will appear, and it will flourish and prosper, and great will be its peace, for "out of the heart are the issues of life."

## Searching for a Solution

Having found that selfishness is the root cause of all competition and strife, the question naturally arises as to how this cause shall be dealt with, for it naturally follows that a cause being destroyed, all its effects cease; a cause being propagated, all its effects, however they may be modified from without, *must* continue.

Every man who has thought at all deeply upon the problem of life, and has brooded sympathetically upon the sufferings of mankind, has seen that selfishness is at the root of all sorrow—in fact, this is one of the truths that is first apprehended by the thoughtful mind. And along with that perception there has been born within him a longing to formulate some methods by which that selfishness might be overcome.

The first impulse of such a man is to endeavor to frame some outward law, or introduce some new social arrangements or regulations, which shall put a check on *the selfishness of others*.

The second tendency of his mind will be to feel his utter helplessness before the great iron will of selfishness by which he is confronted.

Both these attitudes of mind are the result of an incomplete knowledge of what constitutes selfishness. And this partial knowledge dominates him because, although he has overcome the grosser forms of selfishness in himself, and is so far noble, he is yet selfish in other and more remote and subtle directions.

This feeling of "helplessness" is the prelude to one of two conditions—the man will either give up in despair, and again sink himself in the selfishness of the world, or he will search and meditate until he finds another way out of the difficulty. And that way he will find. Looking deeper and ever deeper into the things of life; reflecting, brooding, examining, and analyzing; grappling with every difficulty and problem with intensity of thought, and developing day by day a profounder love of Truth—by these means his heart will grow and his comprehension expand, and at last he will realize that the way to destroy selfishness is not to try to destroy *one form* of it in other people, but to destroy it utterly, root and branch, *in himself.*

The perception of this truth constitutes spiritual illumination, and when once it is awakened in the mind, the "straight and narrow way" is revealed, and the Gates of the Kingdom already loom in the distance.

Then does a man apply to himself (not to others) these words—*And why beholdest thou the mote that is in thy brother's eye, but considerest not the beam that is in thy own eye? Or how wilt thou say to thy brother, let me pull out the mote out of thine eye; and, behold, a beam is in thine own eye? Thou hypocrite, first cast out the beam out of thine own eye; and then shalt thou see clearly to cast out the mote out of thine brother's eye.*

When a man can apply these words to himself and act upon them, judging himself mercilessly, but judging none other, then will he find his way out of the hell of competitive strife, then will he rise above and render of non-effect the laws of competition, and will find the higher Law of Love, subjecting himself to which every evil thing will flee from him, and the joys and blessings which the selfish vainly seek will constantly wait upon him. And not only this, he will, having lifted himself, lift the world. By his example many will see the Way, and will walk it; and the powers of darkness will be weaker for having lived.

### Divine Order is Perfect

It will here be asked, "But will not man who has risen above his selfishness, and therefore above the competitive strife, suffer through the selfishness and competition of those around him? Will he not after all the trouble he has taken to purify himself, suffer at the hands of the impure?"

No, he will not. The equity of the Divine Order is perfect, and cannot be subverted, so that it is impossible for one who has overcome selfishness to be subject to those laws which are brought into operation by the action of selfishness; in other words, each individual suffers by virtue of his own selfishness.

It is true that the selfish all come under the operation of the competitive laws, and suffer collectively, each acting, more or less, as the instrument by which the suffering of others is brought about, which makes it appear, on the surface, as though men suffered for the sins of others rather than their own. But the truth is that in a universe the very basis of which is harmony, and which can only be sustained by the perfect adjustment of all its parts, each unit receives *its own* measure of adjustment, and suffers by and of itself.

Each man comes under the laws of his own being, never under those of another. True, he will suffer like another, and even through the instrumentality of another, if he elects to live under the same conditions as that other. But if he chooses to desert those conditions and to live under another and higher set of conditions of which that other is ignorant, he will cease to come under, or be affected by, the lower laws.

### Selfishness Thrives in Ignorance

Let us now go back to the symbol of the tree and carry the analogy a little further. Just as the leaves and branches are sustained by the roots, so the roots derive their nourishment from the soil, groping blindly in the darkness for the sustenance which the tree demands. In like manner, selfishness, the root of the tree of evil and of suffering, derives its nourishment from the dark soil of *ignorance*. In this it thrives; upon this it stands and flourishes. By ignorance I mean something vastly different from lack of learning; and the sense in which I use it will be made plain as I proceed.

Selfishness always gropes in the dark. It has no knowledge; by its very nature it is cut off from the source of enlightenment; it is a blind impulse, knowing nothing, obeying no law, for it knows none, and is thereby forcibly bound to those competitive laws by virtue of which suffering is inflicted in order that harmony may be maintained.

We live in a world, a universe, abounding with all good things. So great is the abundance of spiritual, mental and material blessings that every man and woman on this globe could not only be provided with every necessary good, but could live in the midst of abounding plenty, and yet have much to spare. Yet, in spite of this, what a spectacle of ignorance do we behold!

We see on the one hand millions of men and women chained to a ceaseless slavery, interminably toiling in order to obtain a poor and scanty meal and a garment to cover their nakedness; and on the other hand we see thousands, who already have more than they require and can well manage, depriving themselves of all the blessings of a true life and of the vast opportunities which their possessions place within their reach, in order to accumulate more of those material things for which they have no legitimate use. Surely men and women have no more wisdom than the beasts which fight over the possession of that which is more than they can all well dispose of, and which they could all enjoy in peace!

Such a condition of things can only occur in a state of ignorance deep and dark; so dark and dense as to be utterly impenetrable save to the unselfish eye of wisdom and truth. And in the midst of all this striving after place and food and raiment, there works unseen, yet potent and unerring, the Overruling Law of Justice, meting out to every individual his own quota of merit and demerit. It is impartial; it bestows no favors; it inflicts no unearned punishments:

> *It knows not wrath nor pardon; utter-true*
> *It measures mete, its faultless balance weighs;*
> *Times are as nought, tomorrow it will judge,*
> *Or after many days.*

### Selfishness Breeds Insecurity

The rich and the poor alike suffer for *their own selfishness*; and none escapes. The rich have their particular sufferings as well as the poor. Moreover, the rich are continually losing their riches; the poor are continually acquiring them. The poor man of today is the rich man of tomorrow, and *vice versa*.

There is no stability, no security in hell, and only brief and occasional periods of respite from suffering in some form or other. Fear, also, follows men like a great shadow, for the man who obtains and holds by selfish force will always be haunted by a feeling of insecurity, and will continually fear its loss; while the poor man, who is selfishly seeking or coveting material riches, will be harassed by the fear of destitution. And one and all who live in this underworld of strife are overshadowed by one great fear—the fear of death.

### The Essential Things of Life

Surrounded by the darkness of ignorance, and having no knowledge of those eternal and life-sustaining Principles out of which all things proceed, men labor under the delusion that the most important and essential things in life are food and clothing, and that their first duty is to strive to obtain these, believing that these outward things are the source and cause of all comfort and happiness.

It is the blind animal instinct of self-preservation (the preservation of the body and personality), by virtue of which each man opposes himself to other men in order to "get a living" or "secure a competency," believing that if he does not keep an incessant watch on other men, and constantly renew the struggle, they will ultimately "take the bread out of his mouth."

It is out of this initial delusion that comes all the train of delusions, with their attendant sufferings. Food and clothing are not the *essential* things of life; not the causes of happiness. They are non-essentials, effects, and, as such, proceed by a process of natural law from the essentials, the underlying cause.

The essential things in life are the enduring elements in character—integrity, faith, righteousness, self-sacrifice, compassion, love; and out of these all good things proceed.

Food and clothing, and money are dead effects; there is in them no life, no power except that which we invest with them. They are without vice and virtue, and can neither bless nor harm. Even the body which men believe to be themselves, to which they pander, and which they long to keep, must very shortly be yielded up to the dust. But the higher elements of character are life itself; and to practice these, to trust them, and to live entirely in them, constitutes the Kingdom of Heaven.

The man who says, "I will first of all earn a competence and secure a good position in life, and will then give my mind to those higher things," does not understand these higher things, does not believe them to be higher, for if he did, it would not be possible for him to neglect them. He believes the material outgrowths of life to be the higher, and therefore he seeks them first. He believes money, clothing and position to be of vast and essential importance, righteousness and truth to be at best secondary; for a man always sacrifices that which he believes to be lesser to that which he believes to be greater.

Immediately after a man *realizes* that righteousness is of more importance than the getting of food and clothing, he ceases to strive after the latter, and begins to live for the former. It is here where we come to the dividing line between the two Kingdoms—Hell and Heaven.

## Operating Under the Law of Love

Once a man perceives the beauty and enduring reality of righteousness, his whole attitude of mind toward himself and others and the things within and around him changes. The love of personal existence gradually loses its hold on him; the instinct of self-preservation begins to die, and the practice of self-renunciation takes its place. For the sacrifice of others, or of the happiness of others, for his own good, he substitutes the sacrifice of self and of his own happiness for the good of others. And thus, rising above self, he rises above the competitive strife which is the outcome of self, and above the competitive laws which operate only in the region of self, and for the regulation of its blind impulses.

He is like the man who has climbed a mountain, and thereby risen above all the disturbing currents in the valleys below him. The clouds pour down their rain, the thunders roll and the lightnings flash, the fogs obscure, and the hurricanes uproot and destroy, but they cannot reach him on the calm heights where he stands, and where he dwells in continual sunshine and peace.

In the life of such a man the lower laws cease to operate, and he now comes under the protection of a higher Law—namely, the Law of Love; and, in accordance with his faithfulness and obedience to this Law, will all that is necessary for his well-being come to him at the time when he requires it.

The idea of gaining a position in the world cannot enter his mind, and the external necessities of life, such as money, food and clothing, he scarcely ever thinks about. But, subjecting himself for the good of others, performing all his duties scrupulously and without thinking of reward, and living day by day in the discipline of righteousness, all other things follow at the right time and in the right order.

### "Seek First the Kingdom of God"

Just as suffering and strife inhere in, and spring from, their root cause, selfishness, so blessedness and peace inhere in, and spring from, their root-cause, righteousness. And it is a full and all-embracing blessedness, complete and perfect in every department of life, for that which is morally and spiritually right is physically and materially right.

Such a man is free, for he is freed from all anxiety, worry, fear, despondency, all those mental disturbances which derive their vitality from the elements of self, and he lives in constant joy and peace, and this while living in the very midst of the competitive strife of the world.

Yet, though walking in the midst of Hell, its flames fall back before and around him, so that not one hair of his head can be singed. Though he walks in the midst of the lions of selfish force, for him their jaws are closed and their ferocity is subdued. Though on every hand men are falling around him in the fierce battle of life, he falls not, neither is he dismayed, for no deadly bullet can reach him, no poisoned shaft can pierce the impenetrable armor of his righteousness. Having lost the little, personal, self-seeking life of suffering, anxiety, fear, and want, he has found the illimitable, glorious, self-perfecting life of joy and peace and plenty.

"Therefore take no thought, saying 'What shall we eat?' or, 'What shall we drink?' or, 'Wherewithal shall we be clothed?...' For your heavenly Father knoweth ye have need of all these things. But seek ye first the Kingdom of God, and His Righteousness, and all these things shall be added unto you."

# The Finding
# of a Principle

*Be still, my soul, and know that peace is within*
*Be steadfast, heart, and know that strength divine*
*Belongs to thee; cease thy turmoil, mind,*
*And thou the everlasting rest shall find.*

HOW THEN SHALL A MAN reach the Kingdom? By what process shall he find the light which alone can disperse his darkness? And in what way can he overcome the inward selfishness which is strong, and deeply rooted?

A man will reach the Kingdom by purifying himself, and he can only do this by pursuing a process of self-examination and self-analysis. The selfishness must be discovered and understood before it can be removed. It is powerless to remove itself, neither will it pass away of itself.

Darkness ceases only when light is introduced; so ignorance can only be dispersed by Knowledge; selfishness by Love. Seeing that in selfishness there is no security, no stability, no peace, the whole process of seeking the Kingdom resolves itself into a search for a Principle; a divine and permanent Principle on which a man can stand secure, freed from himself—that is, from the personal element, and from the tyranny and slavery which that personal self exacts and demands.

A man must first of all be willing to lose himself (his self-seeking self) before he can find himself (his Divine Self). He must realize that selfishness is not worth clinging to, that it is a master altogether unworthy of his service, and that divine Goodness alone is worthy to be enthroned in his heart as the supreme master of his life.

### Faith Grows into Knowledge

This means that he must have faith, for without this equipment there can be neither progress nor achievement. He must believe in the desirability of purity, in the supremacy of righteousness, in the sustaining power of integrity; he must ever hold before him the Ideal and Perfect Goodness, and strive for its achievement with ever-renewed effort and unflagging zeal.

This faith must be nurtured and its development encouraged. As a lamp, it must be carefully trimmed and fed and kept burning in the heart, for without its radiating flame no way will be seen in the darkness; he will find no pathway out of self. And as this flame increases and burns with a steadier light, energy, resolution, and self-reliance will come to his aid, and with each step, his progress will be accelerated until at last the Light of Knowledge will begin to take the place of the lamp of faith, and the darkness will commence to disappear before its searching splendor.

Into his spiritual sight will come the Principles of the divine Life, and as he approaches them, their incomparable beauty and majestic symmetry will astonish his vision, and gladden his heart with a gladness hitherto unknown.

### The Three Gateways of Surrender

Along this pathway of self-control and self-purification (for such it is) every soul must travel on its way to the Kingdom. So narrow is this way, and so overgrown with the weeds of selfishness is its entrance, that it is difficult to find, and, being found, cannot be retained except by *daily meditation*. Without this the spiritual energies grow weaker, and the man loses the strength necessary to continue. As the body is sustained and invigorated by material food, so the spirit is strengthened and renewed by its own food—namely meditation upon spiritual things.

He, then, who earnestly resolves to find the Kingdom will commence to meditate, and to rigidly examine his heart and mind and life in the light of that Supreme Perfection which is the goal of his attainment.

On his way to that goal, he must pass through *three Gateways of Surrender*. The first is *the Surrender of Desire*; the second is *the Surrender of Opinion*; the third is *the Surrender of Self*. Entering into meditation, he will commence to examine his desires, tracing them out in his mind, and following up their effects in his life and upon his character; and he will quickly perceive that, without the renunciation of desire, a man remains a slave both to himself and to his surroundings and circumstances. Having discovered this, the first Gate, that of *the Surrender of Desire*, is entered. Passing through this Gate, he adopts a process of self-discipline which is the first step in the purification of the soul.

## Relinquishing Desire

Hitherto he has lived as a slavish beast; eating, drinking, sleeping, and pursuing enjoyment at the beck and call of his lower impulses; blindly following and gratifying his inclinations without method, not questioning his conduct, and having no fixed center from which to regulate his character and life.

Now, however, he begins to live as a man; he curbs his inclinations, controls his passions, and steadies his mind in the practice of virtue. He ceases to pursue enjoyment, but follows the dictates of his reason, and regulates his conduct in accordance with the demands of an ideal. With the introduction of this regulating factor in his life, he at once perceives that certain habits must be abandoned.

He begins to select his food, and to have his meals at stated periods, no longer eating at any time when the sight of food tempts his inclination. He reduces the number of meals per day and also the quantity of food eaten.

He no longer goes to bed, by day or night, to indulge in pleasurable indolence, but to give his body the rest it needs, and he therefore regulates his hours of sleep, rising early, and never encouraging the animal desire to indulge in dreamy indolence after waking.

All those foods and drinks which are particularly associated with gluttony, cruelty, and drunkenness he will dispense with altogether, selecting the mild and refreshing sustenance which Nature provides in such rich profusion.

These preliminary steps will be at once adopted; and as the path of self-government and self-examination is pursued, a clearer and ever clearer perception of the nature, meaning, and effects of desire will be developed, until it will be seen that the mere regulation of one's desires is altogether inadequate and insufficient, and that *the desires themselves must be abandoned*, must be allowed to fall out of the mind and to have no part in the character and life.

### Entering the Valley of Temptation

It is at this point where the soul of the seeker will enter the dark Valley of Temptation, for these desires will not die without a struggle, and without many a fierce effort to reassert the power and authority with which they have hitherto been invested. And here the lamp of faith must be constantly fed and assiduously trimmed, for all the light that it can throw out will be required to guide and encourage the traveler in the dense gloom of this dark Valley.

At first his desires, like so many wild beasts, will clamor loudly for gratification. Failing in that, they will tempt him to struggle with them that they may overthrow him. And this last temptation is greater and more difficult to overcome than the first, for *the desires will not be stilled until they are utterly ignored*; until they are left unheeded, unconditionally abandoned, and allowed to perish for want of food.

In passing through this Valley, the searcher will develop certain powers which are necessary to his further development, and these powers are—*self-control, self-reliance, fearlessness, and independence of thought*.

Here also he will have to pass through ridicule and mockery and false accusation; so much so, that some of his best friends, yea, even those whom he most unselfishly loves, will accuse him of folly and inconsistency, and will do all they can to argue him back to the life of animal indulgence, self-seeking, and petty personal strife.

Nearly everybody around him will suddenly discover that they know his duty better than he knows it himself, and, knowing no other and higher life than their own of mingled excitement and suffering, they will take great pains to win him back to it, imagining, in their ignorance, that he is losing so much pleasure and happiness, and is gaining nothing in return.

At first this attitude of others toward him will arouse in him acute suffering; but he will rapidly discover that this suffering is caused by his own vanity and selfishness, and is the result of his own subtle desire to be appreciated, admired, and thought well of; and immediately this knowledge is arrived at, he will rise into a higher state of consciousness, where these things can no longer reach him and inflict pain. It is here where he will begin to stand firm, and to wield with effect the powers of mind already mentioned.

Let him therefore press on courageously, heeding neither the revilings of his friends without nor the clamorings of his enemies within; aspiring, searching, striving; looking ever toward his Ideal with eyes of holy love; day by day ridding his mind of selfish motive, his heart of impure desire; stumbling sometimes, sometimes falling, but ever traveling onward and rising higher; and, recording each night in the silence of his own heart the journey of the day, let him not despair if but each day, in spite of all its failures and falls, record some holy battle fought, though lost, some silent victory attempted, though unachieved.

The loss of today will add to the gain of tomorrow for him whose mind is set on the conquest of self.

## Climbing Out of the Valley

Passing along the Valley, he will at last come to the Fields of Sorrow and Loneliness. His desires, having received at his hands neither encouragement nor sustenance, have grown weak, and are now falling away and perishing. He is climbing out of the Valley, and the darkness is less dense; but now he realizes for the first time he is alone. He is like a man standing upon the lowest level of a great mountain, and it is night. Above him towers the lofty peak, beyond which shine the everlasting stars; a short distance below him are the glaring lights of the city which he has left, and from it there come up to him the noises of its inhabitants—a confused mingling of shouts, screams, laughter, rumblings of traffic, and the strains of music. He thinks of his friends, all of whom are in the city, pursuing their own particular pleasures, and he is alone upon the mountain.

That city is the City of Desire and Pleasure, the mountain is the Mountain of Renunciation, and the climber now knows that he has left the world, that henceforth for him its excitements and strifes are lifeless things, and can tempt him no more. Resting awhile in this lonely place, he will taste of sorrow and learn its secret; harshness and hatred will pass from him; his heart will grow soft, and the first faint broodings of that divine compassion, which shall afterwards absorb his whole being, will overshadow and inspire him. He will begin to feel with every living thing in its strivings and sufferings, and gradually, as this lesson is learned, his own sorrow and loneliness will be forgotten in his great calm love for others, and will pass away.

Here, also, he will begin to perceive and understand the workings of those hidden laws which govern the destinies of individuals and nations. Having risen above the lower region of strife and selfishness within himself, he can now look calmly down upon it in others and in the world, and analyze and comprehend it, and he will see how selfish striving is at the root of all the world's suffering.

His whole attitude toward others and the world now undergoes a complete change, and compassion and love begin to take the place of self-seeking and self-protection in his mind; and as a result of this, the world alters in its attitude toward him.

At this juncture he perceives the folly of competition, and, ceasing from striving to overtop and get the better of others, he begins to encourage them, both with unselfish thoughts, and, when necessary, with loving acts; and this he does even to those who selfishly compete with him, no longer defending himself against them.

## Passing Beyond the Fields of Sorrow

As a direct result of this, his worldly affairs begin to prosper as never before; many of his friends who at first mocked him commence to respect, and even to love him, and he suddenly wakes up to the fact that he is coming in contact with people of a distinctly unworldly and noble type, of whose existence he had no knowledge while living in his lower selfish nature. From many parts and from long distances these people will come to him to minister to him and that he may minister to them, spiritual fellowship and loving brotherhood will become potent in his life, and so he will pass beyond the Fields of Sorrow and Loneliness.

The lower competitive laws have now ceased to operate in his life, and their results, which are *failure, disaster, exposure, and destitution*, can no longer enter into and form part of his experience; and this not merely because he has risen above the lower forms of selfishness in himself, but because also, in so rising, he has developed certain power of mind by which he is enabled to direct and govern his affairs with a more powerful and masterly hand.

He, however, has not yet traveled far, and unless he exercises constant watchfulness, may at any time fall back into the lower world of darkness and strife, revivifying its empty pleasures and galvanizing back to life its dead desires. And especially is there danger when he reaches the greatest temptation through which man is called to pass—*the temptation of doubt.*

### The Desert of Doubt

Before reaching, or even perceiving, the second Gate, that of *Surrender of Opinion*, the pilgrim will come upon a great soul-desert, the Desert of Doubt. And here for a time he will wander around, and despondency, indecision, and uncertainty, a melancholy brood, will surround him like a cloud, hiding from his view the way immediately in front of him.

A new and strange fear, too, will possibly overtake him, and he will begin to question the wisdom of the course he is pursuing. Again the allurements of the world will be presented to him, dressed in their most attractive garb, and the drowning din and stimulating excitement of worldly battle will once more assume a desirable aspect.

"After all, am I right? What gain is there in this? Does not life itself consist of pleasure and excitement and battle, and in giving these up am I not giving up all? Am I not sacrificing the very substance of life for a meaningless shadow? May it not be that, after all, I am a poor deluded fool, and that all these around me who live the life of the senses and stand upon its solid, sure, and easily procured enjoyments are wiser than I?"

By such dark doubtings and questionings will he here be tempted and troubled, and these very doubts will drive him to a deeper searching into the intricacies of life, and arouse within him the feeling of necessity for some permanent Principle upon which to stand and take refuge.

He will therefore, while wandering about in this dark Desert, come into contact with the higher and more subtle delusions of his own mind, the delusions of the intellect; and, by contrasting these with his Ideal, will learn to distinguish between the real and the unreal, the shadow and the substance, between effect and cause, between fleeting appearances and permanent Principles.

In the Desert of Doubt a man is confronted with all forms of illusion, not only the illusions of the senses, but also those of abstract thought and religious emotion. It is in the testing of, grappling with, and ultimately destroying, these illusions that he develops still higher powers, those of *discrimination, spiritual perception, steadfastness of purpose*, and *calmness of mind*, by the exercise of which he is enabled to unerringly distinguish the true from the false, both in the world of thought and that of material appearances.

Having acquired these powers, and learned how to use them in his holy warfare as weapons against himself, he now emerges from the Desert of Doubt, the mists and mirages of delusion vanish from his pathway, and there looms before him the second Gate, the *Gateway of the Surrender of Opinion*.

As he approaches this Gate, he sees before him the whole pathway along which he is traveling, and, for a space, obtains a glimpse of the glorious heights of attainment toward which he is moving; he sees the Temple of the Higher Life in all its majesty, and already he feels within him the strength and joy and peace of conquest. With Sir Galahad he can now exclaim:

*"I....saw the Grail,*
*The Holy Grail....*
*....And one will crown me king*
*Far in the spiritual city,"*
for he knows that his ultimate victory is assured.

## *Adjusting Your Thoughts to Principle*

He now enters upon a process of self-conquest, which is altogether distinct from that which he has hitherto pursued. Up to the present he has been overcoming, transmuting, and simplifying his animal desires; now he commences to transmute and simplify his intellect. He has, so far, been adjusting his *feelings* to his Ideals; he now begins to adjust his *thoughts* to that Ideal, which also assumes at this point larger and more beautiful proportions, and for the first time he perceives what really constitutes *a permanent and imperishable Principle*.

He sees that the righteousness for which he has been searching is fixed and invariable; that it cannot be accommodated to man, but that man must reach up to, and obey it; that it consists of an undeviating line of conduct, apart from all considerations of loss or gain, of reward of punishment; that, in reality, it consists in abandoning self, with all the sins of desire, opinion, and self-interest of which that self is composed, and in living the blameless life of perfect love toward all men and creatures. Such a life is fixed and perfect; it is without turning, change, or qualification, and demands a sinless and perfect conduct. It is, therefore, the direct antithesis of the worldly life of self.

Perceiving this, the seeker sees that, although he has freed himself from the baser passions and desires which enslave mankind, he is still in bondage to the fetters of opinion; that although he has purified himself with a purity to which few aspire, and which the world cannot understand, he is still defiled with a defilement which is difficult to wash away—*he loves his own opinions*, and has all along been confounding them with Truth, with the Principle for which he is seeking.

He is not yet free from strife, and is still involved in the competitive laws as they occur in the higher realm of thought. He still believes that he (in his opinions) is right, and that others are wrong; and in his egotism, has even fallen so low as to bestow a mock pity on those who hold opinions the reverse of his own. But now, realizing this more subtle form of selfishness with which he is enslaved, and perceiving all the train of sufferings which spring from it, having also acquired the priceless possession of spiritual discernment, he reverently bends his head and passes through the second Gateway toward his final peace.

## All Opinions Are Worthless

And now, clothing his soul with the colorless Garment of Humility, he bends all his energies to the uprooting of those opinions which he has hitherto loved and cherished.

He now learns to distinguish between Truth, which is one and unchangeable, and his own and others' opinions about Truth, which are many and changeable.

He sees that his *opinions* about Goodness, Purity, Compassion, and Love are very distinct from those qualities themselves, and that he must stand upon those divine Principles, and not upon his opinions. Hitherto he has regarded his own opinions as of great value, and the opinions of others as worthless, but now he ceases to so elevate his own opinions and to defend them against those of others, and comes to regard them as utterly worthless.

## The Joy of No Opinion

As a direct result of this attitude of mind, he

takes refuge in the practice of *pure Goodness*, unalloyed with base desire and subtle self-love, and takes his stand upon the divine Principles of Purity, Wisdom, Compassion, and Love, incorporating them into his mind, and manifesting them in his life.

He is now clothed with *the Righteousness of Christ* (which is incomprehensible to the world) and is rapidly becoming divine. He has not only realized the darkness of desire; he has also perceived the vanity of speculative philosophy, and so rids his mind of all those metaphysical subtleties which have no relation to practical holiness, and which hitherto encumbered his progress and prevented him from seeing the enduring realities in life.

And now he casts from him, one after another, his opinions and speculations, and commences to live the life of perfect love toward all beings. With each opinion overcome and abandoned as a burden, there is an increased lightness of spirit, and he now begins to realize the meaning of being "free."

The divine flowers of Gladness, Joy, and Peace spring up spontaneously in his heart, and his life becomes a blissful song. And as the melody in his heart expands, and grows more and more perfect, his outward life harmonizes itself with the inward music.

All the effort he puts forth being now free from strife, he obtains all that is necessary for his well-being, without pain, anxiety, or fear. He has almost entirely transcended the competitive laws, and the Law of Love is now the governing factor in his life, adjusting all his worldly affairs harmoniously, and without struggle or difficulty on his part.

Indeed, the competitive laws as they occur in the commercial world, have been long left behind, and have ceased to touch him at any point in his material affairs. Here, also, he enters into a wider and more comprehensive consciousness, and viewing the universe and humanity from the higher altitudes of purity and knowledge to which he has ascended, perceives the orderly sequence of law in all human affairs.

### The End of Anguish

The pursuit of this Path brings about the development of still higher powers of mind, and these powers are—*divine patience, spiritual equanimity, non-resistance, and prophetic insight.* By prophetic insight I do not mean, the foretelling of events, but direct perception of those hidden causes which operate in human life, and, indeed, in all life, and out of which spring the multifarious and universal effects and events.

The man here rises above the competitive laws as they operate in the thought world, so that their results, which are *violence, ignominy, grief, humiliation* and *distress* and *anxiety* in all their forms, no longer occur in his life.

As he proceeds, the imperishable Principles which form the foundation and fabric of the universe loom before him, and assume more and more symmetrical proportions. For him there is no more anguish; no evil can come near his dwelling; and there breaks upon him the dawning of the abiding Peace.

But he is not yet free. He has not yet finished his journey. He may rest here, and that as long as he chooses; but sooner or later he will rouse himself to the last effort, and will reach the final goal of achievement—the selfless state, the divine life.

He is not yet free from self, but still clings, though with less tenacity, to the love of personal existence, and to the idea of exclusive interest in his personal possessions. And when he at last realizes that those selfish elements must also be abandoned, there appears before him the third Gate—*the Gateway of Surrender of Self.*

## The Last Great Gate of Glory

It is no dark portal which he now approaches, but one luminous with divine glory, one radiant with a radiance with which no earthly splendor can vie, and he advances toward it with no uncertain step. The clouds of Doubt have long been dispersed; the sounds of the voices of Temptation are lost in the valley below; and with firm gait, erect carriage, and a heart filled with unspeakable joy, he nears the Gate that guards the Kingdom of God.

He has now given up all but self-interest in those things which are his by legal right, but he now perceives that he must hold nothing as his own; and as he pauses at the Gate, he hears the command which cannot be evaded or denied: "Yet lackest thou one thing; sell all that thou hast, and distribute unto the poor, and thou shall have treasure in Heaven."

And passing through the last great Gate, he stands glorious, radiant, free, detached from the tyranny of desire, of opinion, of self; a divine man— harmless, patient, tender, pure; he has found that for which he had been searching—the Kingdom of God and His Righteousness.

## *All Who Believe Will Arrive*

The journey to the Kingdom may be a long and tedious one, or it may be short and rapid. It may occupy a minute, or it may take a thousand ages. Everything depends on the faith and belief of the searcher. The majority cannot "enter in because of their unbelief"; for how can men realize righteousness when they do not believe in it nor in the possibility of its accomplishment?

Neither is it necessary to leave the outer world, and one's duties therein. Nay, it can only be found through the unselfish performance of one's duty. Some there are whose faith is so great that, when this truth is presented to them, they can let all the personal elements drop almost immediately out of their minds, and enter into their divine heritage.

But all who believe and aspire to achieve will sooner or later arrive at victory if, amid all their worldly duties, they faint not, nor lose sight of the Ideal Goodness, and continue, with unshaken resolve to "press on to Perfection."

# At Rest in the Kingdom
# & All Things Are Added

THE WHOLE JOURNEY from the Kingdom of Strife to the Kingdom of Love resolves itself into a process which may be summed up in the following words: *The regulation and purification of conduct*. Such a process must, if assiduously pursued, necessarily lead to perfection. It will also be seen that as the man obtains the mastery over certain forces within himself, he arrives at a knowledge of all the laws which operate in the realm of those forces, and by watching the ceaseless working of cause and effect within himself, until he understands it, he then understands it in its universal adjustments in the body of humanity.

Moreover, seeing that all the laws which govern human affairs are the direct outcome of the necessities of the human heart, he, having reformed and transmuted those necessities, has brought himself under the guidance of other laws which operate in accordance with the altered condition, and that, having mastered and overcome the selfish forces within himself, he can no longer be subject to the laws which exist for their governance.

The process is also one of *simplification of the mind*, a sifting away of all but the essential gold in character. And as the mind is thus simplified, the apparently unfathomable complexity of the universe assumes simpler and simpler aspects, until the whole is seen to resolve itself into, and rest upon, a few unalterable Principles; and these Principles are ultimately seen to be contained in *one*, namely LOVE.

## Compassion for Others

The mind thus simplified, the man arrives at peace, and he now really begins to *live*. Looking back on the personal life which he has forever abandoned, he sees it as a horrible nightmare out of which he has awakened; but looking out and down with the eyes of the spirit, he sees that others continue to live it. He sees men and women struggling, fighting, suffering and perishing for that which is abundantly given to them by the bountiful hand of the Father, if they would only cease from all covetousness, and take it without hurt or hindrance;

and compassion fills his heart, and also gladness, for he knows that humanity will wake at last from its long and painful dream.

In the early part of the journey he seemed to be leaving humanity far behind, and he sorrowed in his loneliness. But now, having reached the highest, having attained the goal, he finds himself nearer to humanity than ever before—yea, living in its very heart, sympathizing with all its sorrows, rejoicing in all its joys; for, having no longer any personal considerations to defend, he lives entirely in the heart of humanity.

He lives no longer for himself; he lives for others; and so living, he enjoys the highest bliss, the deepest peace.

For a time he searched for Compassion, Love, Bliss, Truth; but now he has verily become Compassion, Love, Bliss, Truth; and it may literally be said of him that he has ceased to be a personality, for all the personal elements have been extinguished, and there remain only those qualities and principles which are entirely impersonal. And those qualities are now manifested in the man's life, and henceforth the man's character.

And having ceased from the protection of the

self, and living constantly in compassion, wisdom and love, he comes under the protection of the highest Law, the Law of Love; and he understands that Law, and consciously co-operates with it; yea, is himself inseparately identified with the Law.

## Principles Are the Eternal Reality

"Forgoing self, the universe grows I": and he whose nature is compassion, wisdom and love cannot possibly need any protection; for those Principles themselves constitute the highest protection, being the real, the divine, the immortal in all men and women, and constituting the indestructible reality in the cosmic order.

Neither does he need to seek enjoyment whose very nature is Bliss, Joy, Peace. As for competing with others, with whom should he compete who has lovingly identified himself with all? With whom should he struggle who has sacrificed himself for all? Whose blind, misguided, and ineffectual competition should he fear who has reached the source of all blessedness, and who receives at the hands of the Father all necessary things?

Having lost himself (his selfish personality), he has found himself (his divine nature, Love); and Love and all the effects of Love now compose his life. He can now joyfully exclaim—

> *I have made the acquaintance*
> *of the Master of Compassion;*
> *I have put on the Garment of the Perfect Law;*
> *I have entered the realm of the Great Reality;*
> *Wandering is ended, for Rest is accomplished;*
> *Pain and sorrow have ceased,*
> *for Peace is entered into;*
> *Confusion is dissolved, for Unity is made manifest;*
> *Error is vanquished, for Truth is revealed!*

### Love is the One Supreme Law

The Harmonizing Principle, Righteousness, or Divine Love, being found, all things are seen as they are, and not through the illusory mediums of selfishness and opinion; the universe is *One*, and all its manifold operations are the manifestation of *one Law*.

Hitherto in this work *laws* have been referred to, and also spoken of as *higher* and *lower*, and this distinction was necessary; but now the Kingdom is reached, we see that all the forces operative in human life are the varied manifestations of the One Supreme Law of Love. It is by virtue of this Law that Humanity suffers, that, by the intensity of its suffer-

ings, it shall become purified and wise, and so relinquish the source of suffering, which is selfishness.

The Law and foundation of the universe being
Love, it follows that all self-seeking is opposed to
that Law, is an effort to overcome or ignore the Law,
and as a result, every self-seeking act and thought is
followed by an exact quota of suffering which is
required to annul its effect, and so maintain the universal harmony. All suffering is, therefore, the
*restraint* which the Law of Love puts upon ignorance
and selfishness, and out of such painful restraint Wisdom at last emerges.

## The Kingdom of Love Supplies All Needs

There being no strife and no selfishness in the
Kingdom, there is therefore no suffering, no
restraint; there is perfect harmony, equipoise, rest.
Those who have entered it do not follow any animal
inclinations (they have none to follow), but live in
accordance with the highest Wisdom. Their nature is
Love, and they live in love toward all.

They are never troubled about "making a living," as they are Life itself, living in the very Heart
of Life; and should any material or other need arise,
that need is immediately supplied without any anxi-

ety or struggle on their part.

Should they be called to undertake any work, the money and friends needed to carry out that work are immediately forthcoming. Having ceased to violate their principles, all their needs are supplied through legitimate channels. Any money or help required always comes through the instrumentality of good people who are either living in the Kingdom themselves, or are working for its accomplishment.

Those who live in the Kingdom of Love have all their needs supplied by the Law of Love, with all freedom from unrest, just as those who live in the kingdom of self only meet their needs by much strife and suffering. Having altered the root cause in their heart they have altered all the effects in their inner and outer life. As self is the root cause of all strife and suffering, so Love is the root cause of all peace and bliss.

## Being One with God

Those who are at rest in the Kingdom do not look for happiness to any outward possession. They see that all such possessions are mere transient effects that come when they are required, and after their purpose is served, pass away.

They never think of these things (money, clothing, food, etc.) except as mere accessories and *effects* of the true Life. They are therefore freed from all anxiety and trouble, and resting in Love, they are the embodiment of happiness.

Standing upon the imperishable Principles of Purity, Compassion, Wisdom and Love, they are immortal, and know they are immortal; they are one with God (the Supreme Good), and know they are one with God. Seeing the realities of things, they can find no room anywhere for condemnation. All the operations that occur upon the earth they see as instruments of the Good Law, even those called *evil*.

All men are essentially divine, though unaware of their divine nature, and all their acts are efforts, even though many of them are dark and impotent, to realize some higher good. All so-called evil is seen to be rooted in ignorance, even those deeds that are called *deliberately wicked*, so that condemnation ceases, and Love and Compassion become all in all.

### At Rest in the Kingdom

But let it not be supposed that the children of the kingdom live in ease and indolence (these two sins are the first that have to be eradicated when the search for the Kingdom is entered upon); they live in a peaceful activity; in fact, *they only* truly live, for the life of self with its train of worries, griefs, and fears, is not *real* life.

They perform all their duties with the most scrupulous diligence, apart from thoughts of self, and employ all their means, as well as powers and faculties, which are greatly intensified, in building up the Kingdom of Righteousness in the hearts of others and in the world around them. This is their work— first by example, then by precept.

Having sold all that they have (renounced all self-interest in their possessions), they now give to the poor (give of their rich store of wisdom, love and peace to the needy in spirit, the weary and broken-hearted), and follow the Christ whose name is LOVE.

And they have sorrow no more, but live in perpetual gladness, for though they see suffering in the world, they also see the final Bliss and the Eternal Refuge of Love, to which whosoever is ready may come *now*, and to which all will come at last.

## Children of the Kingdom

The children of the Kingdom *are known by their*

*life*. They manifest the fruits of the Spirit—"love, joy, peace, long-suffering, kindness, goodness, faithfulness, meekness, temperance, self-control"—under all circumstances and vicissitudes. They are entirely free from anger, fear, suspicion, jealousy, caprice, anxiety, and grief. Living in the Righteousness of God, they manifest qualities which are the very reverse of those which occur in the world, and which are regarded by the world as foolishness.

They demand no *rights*; they do not defend themselves; do not retaliate; do good to those who attempt to injure them; manifest the same gentle spirit toward those who oppose and attack them as toward those who agree with them; do not pass judgement on others; condemn no person and no system, and live at peace with all.

The Kingdom of Heaven is perfect trust, perfect knowledge, perfect peace. All is music, sweetness, and tranquillity. No irritations, no bad tempers, no harsh words, no suspicions, no lust, and no disturbing elements can enter there.

Its children live in perfect sweetness, forgiving and forgiven, ministering to others with kindly thoughts and words, and deeds. And that Kingdom is in the heart of every man and woman; it is their

rightful heritage, their own Kingdom; theirs to enter *now*. But *no sin can enter therein*; no self-born thought or deed can pass its Golden Gates; no impure desire can defile its radiant robes.

All may enter it who will, but all *must pay the price, and that is—the unconditional abandonment of self.*

"If thou wilt be perfect, sell all that thou hast"; but at these words the world turns away "sorrowful, for it is very rich"; rich in money which it cannot keep; rich in fears which it cannot let go; rich in selfish loves to which it greedily clings; rich in grievous partings which it would fain escape; rich in seeking enjoyment; rich in pain and sorrow; rich in strife and suffering; rich in excitement and woe; rich in all things which are not riches, but poor in riches themselves which are not to be found outside the Kingdom; rich in all things that pertain to darkness and death, but poor in those things which are Light and Life.

He then, who would realize the Kingdom, let him pay the price and enter. If he have a great and holy faith he can do it *now*, and, letting fall from him like a garment the self to which he has been clinging, stand free. If he have less faith, he must rise above self more slowly, and find the Kingdom by daily effort and patient work.

The Temple of Righteousness is built and its four walls are the four Principles—Purity, Wisdom, Compassion, Love. Peace is its roof; its floor Steadfastness, its entrance-door is Selfless Duty, its atmosphere is Inspiration, and its music is the Joy of the perfect.

It cannot be shaken, and, being eternal and indestructible, there is no more need to seek protection in taking thought for the things of tomorrow. And the Kingdom of Heaven being established in the heart, the obtaining of the material necessities of life is no more considered, for, having found the Highest, all these things are added as effect to cause; the struggle for existence has ceased, and the spiritual, mental, and material needs are daily supplied from the universal abundance.

*Long I sought thee, Spirit holy,*
*Master Spirit, meek and lowly;*
*Sought thee with a silent sorrow, brooding over*
*the woes of men;*
*Vainly sought thy yoke of meekness*
*'Neath the weight of woe and weakness;*
*Finding not, yet in my failing, seeking over and*
*over again.*

In unrest and doubt and sadness
Dwelt I, yet I knew thy Gladness
Waited somewhere; somewhere greeted torn and
sorrowing hearts like mine;
Knew that somehow I should find thee,
Leaving sin and woe behind me,
And at last thy Love would bid me enter into
Rest divine.

Hatred, mockery, and reviling
Scorched my seeking soul defiling
That which should have been thy Temple, wherein
thou shouldest move and dwell;
Praying, striving, hoping, calling;
Suffering, sorrowing in my falling,
Still I sought thee, groping blindly, in the gloomy
depths of Hell.

And I sought thee till I found thee;
And the dark powers all around me
Fled, and left me silent, peaceful, brooding ove.
thy holy themes;
From within me and without me
Fled they when I ceased to doubt thee;
And I found thee in thy Glory, mighty Master
of my dreams!

*Yes, I found thee, Spirit holy,*
*Beautiful and pure and lowly;*
*Found thy Joy and Peace and Gladness; found*
*thee in thy House of Rest;*
*Found thy strength in Love and Meekness,*
*And my pain and woe and weakness*
*Left me, and I walked the Pathway trodden only*
*by the blest.*